# A Celebration of God's Unfailing Love

© Evangelical Sisterhood of Mary, 1997
Darmstadt-Eberstadt, Germany

ISBN 3 87209 649 4

Original title: *Gottes Treue durch 50 Jahre Evangelische Marienschwesternschaft 1947-1997*

First German edition 1997
First English edition 1997

Available in Australia from:

> Evangelical Sisterhood of Mary
> 30 Taylor Place, Theresa Park, NSW 2570

Available in Canada from:

> Evangelical Sisterhood of Mary
> 4285 Heritage Drive, Tracy, NB, E0G 3C0
> and: R.R.1, Millet, Alberta, T0C 1Z0

Available in the UK from:

> Evangelical Sisterhood of Mary
> Radlett, Herts. WD7 8DE

Available in the USA from:

> Evangelical Sisterhood of Mary
> P.O. Box 30022, Phoenix, AZ 85046-0022

Printed in Germany

# A Celebration
# of God's Unfailing Love

*Evangelical Sisterhood of Mary*
*1947-1997*

**B**e very
careful
never to forget
what you
have seen God
doing for you.
May his
miracles have a
deep and
permanent effect
upon your
lives!

Deuteronomy 4:9 LB

# 1947–1997

This jubilee book is dedicated in loving gratitude to our founding mothers

Mother Basilea Schlink *(right)*
Mother Martyria Madauss *(left)*

who have led the way for us as a spiritual family throughout these 50 years.

In our day there is an unspoken longing for mothers and fathers in Christ (1 Corinthians 4:15), people who reflect the Saviour, people whose lives point to Him. The Sermon on the Mount is widely considered too utopian to apply to everyday life. Searching questions are asked about coping with suffering and breaking through to the joy of the Lord — a joy no one can take away (John 16:22).

How we thank God for giving us two mothers in Christ who have found the key to these issues and who with their whole being are an open letter from Christ (2 Corinthians 3:3). For many others, too, they have become spiritual mothers, God having used their testimony to touch numerous lives.

Years before the Sisterhood of Mary began, God prepared our founding mothers for their future ministry, leading them to do without any earthly security and to rely completely upon Him. Making God alone their help and refuge in every situation, they grew strong in faith, and thus were enabled later to lead our entire community along the same path.

In retrospect we can only say that as we have walked this path with our mothers God has never disappointed us, for He stands by His word and no one who has faith in God will ever be disgraced for trusting

Him (Psalm 25:3). Over the years each one of us has personally discovered God's heart to be a fount of infinite goodness and mercy.

The Fountain of the Father's Goodness at Kanaan was built as a symbol of His overflowing fatherly love. Seven of the Father's names in mosaic adorn the edge of the fountain. These names will be accompanying us throughout this book, highlighting how God has revealed Himself to us these past 50 years: merciful and gracious, abounding in steadfast love and faithfulness (Exodus 34:6).

In the course of their long lives our mothers have drawn from God's goodness and mercy in everything they believed and prayed for, received and passed on, their one longing being that He would be glorified in the sight of all. As a fellowship, we now face a great challenge. It is our prayer that we will preserve what our mothers laid deep into the foundations of Kanaan and, by the grace of God, continue to build upon these foundations both inwardly and outwardly.

This jubilee book is also dedicated to our friends, who have selflessly placed themselves at God's disposal and assisted in our commission. Without their prayers, sacrifices and efforts, our ministry at Kanaan and in the branches could not have been carried out to such an extent. We are comforted to know that behind every 'Father in heaven, now bless and reward them' is the tremendous reality of God, whose love does not let the smallest sacrifice go unrewarded.

*Kanaan, March 30, 1997     The Sisters of Mary*

1  *Klara Schlink, PhD. (right)*
   *and Erika Madauss (left), 1936*

2  *In 1974*

3  *In 1982*

4  *Mother Martyria with Sisters of the Crown of Thorns*

5  *Mother Basilea with Canaan Franciscan Brothers*

6  *Mother Martyria explaining Grünewald's 'The Crucifixion'*

7  *Mother Basilea with her former school friend, a Sister of Thorns, who served for many years at our praise chapel in Aeschi, Switzerland*

**Y**ou
in your mercy
have led forth
the people
whom you have
redeemed;
you have guided
them in
your strength to
your holy
habitation.

Exodus 15 : 13 RAV

# FATHER OF MERCY

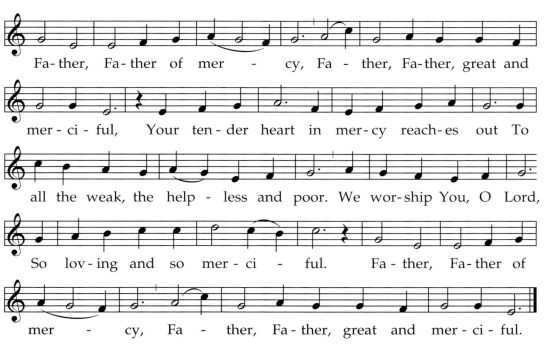

Fa-ther, Fa-ther of mer - cy, Fa - ther, Fa-ther, great and

mer - ci - ful, Your ten-der heart in mer-cy reach-es out To

all the weak, the help - less and poor. We wor-ship You, O Lord,

So lov-ing and so mer-ci - ful. Fa-ther, Fa-ther of

mer - cy, Fa - ther, Fa-ther, great and mer-ci - ful.

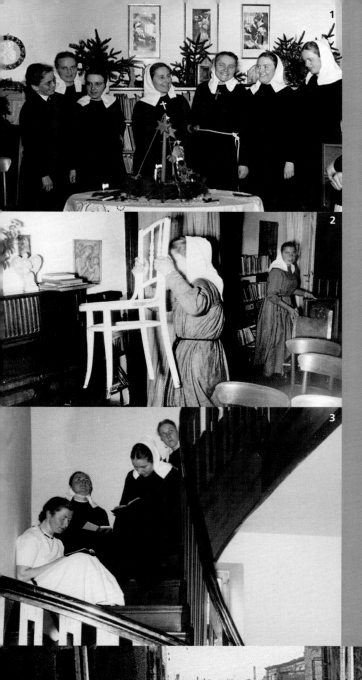

# New Life from Ashes

SEPTEMBER 11, 1944: Darmstadt is destroyed in an air-raid; over 12,000 are dead…For years our mothers had prayed for revival in the girls' Bible study groups they led; now their prayers were answered — far differently than they had ever expected. That night the girls encountered God in His holiness as Judge and Lord over life and death. Nothing could be hidden, no lukewarm Christianity could stand in His holy presence.

Following that night of terror, there was a move among those young girls to bring sin into the light and receive forgiveness. 'Where there is forgiveness of sins, there is also life and salvation' (Martin Luther). God's moment had come. Out of the ashes emerged new life.

MARCH 30, 1947: Inaugural ceremony of the Sisterhood of Mary in the home of Mother Basilea's parents, Steinberg House, which had largely escaped the bombing. Soon God would lead the group of young sisters out of the narrow confines of a one-family home into a larger property and eventually their own 'Promised Land', Kanaan, named after the biblical Canaan because it would be acquired by faith alone.

1   Steinberg House, December 1949
2-3 Bursting at the seams
4-5 Darmstadt, 1945
6   Mother Basilea's parents, Steinberg House
7   Herald Chapel

10

6

# Repentance Is the Gateway

TUT
BUSSE
DAS
HIMMEL-
REICH
IST
NAHE

Even to passing motorists on the Heidelberger Landstrasse, Kanaan's entrance monument stands out with its unusual inscription: 'Repent, for the kingdom of heaven is at hand' (Matthew 4:17). This, the core of Jesus' message, also sums up the Rule of our community life. Repentance is not a one-time act: it involves a daily 'about-turn', a daily turning away from our sinful ways.

Today, after 50 years, we can testify that repentance was each time the gateway to a fresh experience of God's grace. As in the parable of the prodigal son, repentance leads to joyful celebration (Luke 15). And this gateway remains open for us daily, His mercies being new every morning (Lamentations 3:22-23).

'Your kingdom come' — this request in the Lord's prayer has always been a concern close to the hearts of our mothers. How Jesus longed for the

dawning of His kingdom, for something of it to become visible among His followers, so that the world might believe (John 17:20-23). But for this longing of Jesus to be fulfilled, daily repentance is crucial. Aware of our own sin and need of forgiveness, we learn to forgive others. Thus love for Jesus and for one another grows — a foreshadowing of heaven.

Our mothers clung unswervingly to this as a goal of faith, reaffirming their stand on God's Word after every disappointment. This is harder than acquiring a piece of land against overwhelming odds, harder than building without the necessary funds, harder than carrying out a worldwide ministry. But what costs most is worth most.

1  *Our future Kanaan*
2  *Entrance monument*
3  *Procession at Kanaan*
4  *Sea of Galilee and Herald Chapel*

# In Honour of the Living God

Just as in Ancient Rome there was a Via Triumphalis, so, too, at Kanaan there is a Triumphal Way — not for some victorious general but in honour of the living God, commemorating His mighty deeds.

It was God who gave Mother Basilea the assurance in her heart that He would need the adjoining grounds south of the Mother House for a new ministry. Kanaan was to be a place of prayer and quiet, of reconciliation, love and peace, a land of joyful celebration.

However, the response to our mothers' initial inquiries could not have been less encouraging: Quarters for American officers were to be built on the site, construction beginning in two weeks' time. A bypass had long been planned. And what looked like one piece of land had, in fact, many owners: the state, the city, the church,

and some 20 individuals and their heirs. For God, humanly impossible situations are ideal conditions for Him to act. But for our young sisterhood, it meant embarking on a venture of faith contrary to human reason and incurring scepticism from others. That was inevitable if God alone was to receive the glory — and He did, sovereignly bringing everything to a successful conclusion.

When the children of Israel had crossed the River Jordan to possess the land, the Lord commanded them to set up twelve memorial stones, a reminder to future generations of the mighty deeds of God (Joshua 4). The stones flanking Kanaan's Triumphal Way serve the same purpose, briefly chronicling the remarkable intervention of God in many near-impossible situations.

MAY WE SHOUT FOR JOY OVER YOUR VICTORY, AND IN THE NAME OF OUR GOD SET UP OUR BANNERS! MAY THE LORD FULFIL ALL YOUR PETITIONS! — PSALM 20:

Scripture received in prayer for a decisive talk with the Chief City Engineer on June 1, 1955, as part of the preliminaries for the acquisition of Kanaan. The city had completely different plans for the land; yet, unbelievably, the Chief City Engineer took our plea to heart and supported us in our quest for Kanaan.

DO NOT LET THEM ENTER THEIR CITIES; FOR THE LORD YOUR GOD HAS GIVEN THEM INTO YOUR HAND. JOSHUA 10:19

Verse received on May 4, 1955, for what seemed an impossible project: to acquire Kanaan for God's ministry, although the land had already been designated for other purposes. However, God's hand was upon it and He miraculously intervened. No one can withstand a commission of God.

FEAR NOT, YOU WORM JACOB, YOU MEN OF ISRAEL! I WILL HELP YOU, SAYS THE LORD. ISAIAH 41:14

God's promise in June 1955 when the way to Kanaan was completely blocked. Numerous visits to the municipal authorities only resulted in our requests being categorically turned down. But God proved Himself our helper, repeatedly raising up people to join us in the struggle to acquire Kanaan.

WHAT FATHER AMONG YOU, IF HIS SON ASKS FOR BREAD, WILL GIVE HIM A STONE; OR IF HE ASKS FOR A FISH, WILL INSTEAD OF A FISH GIVE HIM A SERPENT? LUKE 11:11

June 27, 1955 — a crushing blow! No relocation of the government-planned bypass through the middle of our prospective Kanaan — and that was final! However, the Father in heaven kept His promise. He would not give a stone instead of bread, that is, noisy traffic instead of peace and quiet and sufficient space for His ministry. February 8, 1956, brought the news that the bypass would be relocated after all!

**HE FOUND HIM ... IN THE HOWLING WASTE OF THE WILDERNESS; HE ENCIRCLED HIM, HE CARED FOR HIM, HE KEPT HIM AS THE APPLE OF HIS EYE.** DEUTERONOMY 32:10

Scripture received for 1956 when there seemed little prospect of acquiring the various fields and pieces of property of our future Kanaan. It renewed our dedication to following dark paths of faith with the Father's loving, chastening hand upon us. Desert wanderings must be: they alone lead to Kanaan.

**THIS IS THE WAY, WALK IN IT.** ISAIAH 30:21

February 1956 — many voices warned that the venture of faith concerning Kanaan was tempting God. In this time of testing this scripture gave us the strength to follow God's leading to the end.

**THESE PEOPLE ALL TRUSTED GOD AND AS A RESULT ... RECEIVED WHAT GOD HAD PROMISED THEM.** HEBREWS 11:33 LB
**IT IS GOOD BOTH TO HOPE AND WAIT QUIETLY FOR THE SALVATION OF THE LORD.** LAMENTATIONS 3:26 LB

February 1956 — a flat refusal from the state of Hesse ever to sell us land. These promises from the Lord were a comfort and assurance that perseverance in faith would be rewarded.

**IF YOU WILL NOT BELIEVE, SURELY YOU SHALL NOT BE ESTABLISHED.** ISAIAH 7:9

Scripture received in March 1956 concerning the impossibility of acquiring the 20 privately-owned properties of our future Kanaan. Through believing prayer one door after the other opened until, in 1963, the land was available for the Lord and His service.

**HE WHO CALLS YOU IS FAITHFUL, AND HE WILL DO IT.** 1 THESSALONIANS 5:24

This confirmed the Lord's commission to begin building the retreat centre 'Jesus' Joy' in autumn 1956, although we had no land to build on. Through God's marvellous intervention we were guaranteed three acres from the state of Hesse by autumn 1956.

**BEHOLD, I HAVE SET THE LAND BEFORE YOU; GO IN AND TAKE POSSESSION OF THE LAND.** DEUTERONOMY 1

At the beginning of 1957, when there was still no prospec of our acquiring Kanaan in total, this was the verse Go gave the sisterhood as a motto for the year. He wonder fully fulfilled His word, and on March 30, 1957, the tent anniversary of the sisterhood, He gave us a special birth day present: the city council promised us first option t the entire area of our future Kanaan.

**THE LORD YOUR GOD ... LED YOU THROUGH THE GREAT AND TERRIBLE WILDERNESS ... THAT HE MIGHT HUMBLE YOU AND TEST YOU, TO DO YOU GOOD IN THE END.** DEUTERONOMY 8:14-1

Scripture for further wilderness wanderings from 1957 t 1959 when doubts were raised again about allowing u first option. The state of Hesse, which still owned two thirds of the land, declined to accept the property offere in exchange. But God provided a gracious outcome to th long wilderness wanderings: in February 1959, thanks t the tireless efforts of our local mayor, all the state- or city owned property became ours.

**NONE WHO HAVE FAITH IN GOD WILL EVER BE DISGRACED FOR TRUSTING HIM.** PSALM 25:3 L

Scripture received on March 30, 1959, when reviewin the wilderness wanderings, the paths of faith leading t Kanaan. The Lord proved Himself to be Yes and Amer He had kept His word. Kanaan was available for Hi ministry and to glorify His name and fatherly goodness

---

1   Triumphal Way is built

2-3 Giving thanks with our mothers on the Triumphal Way, 1985

4   Entrance monument viewed from inside Kanaan.
    Text: 'God's name is Yes and Amen. His holy name we laud and praise. He does whatever He says.'

16

GOTT HEISSET
JA UND AMEN·
WIR PREISEN
SEINEN NAMEN·
ER TUT/ WAS
ER VERSPRICHT·

4

2

3

17

# How You will help we do not know,
## But that You'll help we know for sure!

## Kanaan
### 1960-1966

This was our song while working. During this period, however, we discovered that God was more concerned with the inner than with the outer structuring of Kanaan. The many obstacles and setbacks He sent were intended to help us, as living stones, to be built into a spiritual house (1 Peter 2:5). As with the earlier building of the Mother House and Chapel, every difficulty we now encountered drove us to prayer and to ask ourselves how we had hindered God from helping. Usually it was those so-called little disagreements which came under the Lord's spotlight. Admittedly, in the Lord's Prayer we pray, 'Forgive us our sins as we forgive those who sin against us.' But the Lord convicted us that we often fail to do just that, insisting we are in the right, holding grudges and judging one another. Only through the repeated practice of forgiveness can the 'cement of love' hold us firmly together as living stones.

1   Herald Chapel
2   Praying for water on the unpaved bed of the lake
3   View of Mount Tabor
4-6 Constructing the Garden of Jesus' Sufferings
7   Drilling for water
8   Landscaping of hills
9   Hedge-planting
10  Garden of Jesus' Sufferings and Jacob's Well

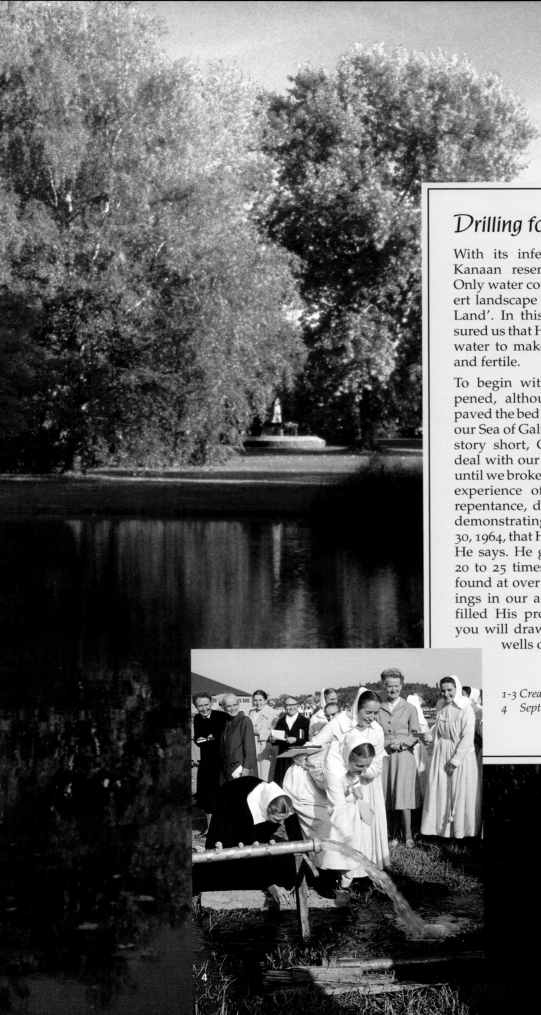

## Drilling for Water

With its infertile sandy soil Kanaan resembled a desert. Only water could turn this desert landscape into a 'Promised Land'. In this plight God assured us that He would provide water to make the land green and fertile.

To begin with, nothing happened, although in faith we paved the bed of what was to be our Sea of Galilee. To cut a long story short, God first had to deal with our hard hearts. Not until we broke through to a new experience of contrition and repentance, did He intervene, demonstrating on September 30, 1964, that He stands by what He says. He gave us water — 20 to 25 times more than that found at over 100 similar drillings in our area! Yes, He fulfilled His promise: 'With joy you will draw water from the wells of salvation'.

Isaiah 12:3

1-3 Creation of Sea of Galilee
4    September 30, 1964

21

# The Great Landscape Gardener

Land, buildings, water — but what about the vegetation? For that, too, the Father had His plan. Every tree and shrub could tell a story, as could our garden sisters. Today, when visitors comment on the fine trees, thick hedgerows, spacious lawns and wealth of roses at Kanaan, we are reminded of how it all began: with a sense of great helplessness.

None of us had any experience in landscape gardening. However, as we had earlier discovered when building the Mother House and Chapel, the heavenly Father has pity on those who trust in Him alone. It was primarily God Himself who took over the landscaping, whether raising up friends to assist or giving Mother Martyria the inspiration as to which tree should be planted where. Once again He glorified Himself among the helpless, and today very often it is professional landscape gardeners who ask in amazement, 'Who did the landscaping so beautifully?'

1    *View of Kanaan looking towards Eberstadt, 1967*

2-3  *A summer's day at Kanaan*

4    *Mount of Beatitudes*

23

Kanaan, our 'Promised Land', is indeed a land where God fulfilled His promises. Learning of what God has done, others are putting their trust in Him for whom nothing is impossible (Luke 1:37). From the very beginning our founding mothers' motivation was: To GOD BE THE GLORY! One and all were to see that 'the Lord is merciful and gracious ... and abounding in steadfast love' (Psalm 103:8). To achieve this they did not shrink from humiliations and setbacks, trials and temptations.

A visitor who hardly knew us put it this way: 'When I set foot on the grounds at Kanaan, I sense this land has been won for God through prayer.' Despite the evil one's attacks, Kanaan has increasingly become an oasis in these troubled times — all thanks to His infinite mercy.

✤

24

*1  In 1976     2  In 1967*

2

25

25

# I WILL REBUKE THE DEVOURER.

Malachi 3:1

**6**

1 *Fire Blight*
2 *Ladybirds devouring lice*
3 *Gypsy Moth caterpillars*
4 *Slugs*
5 *Grubs*
6 *Harvest joy*

In the late 1960s when there was still widespread indifference to the destruction and pollution of the soil, Mother Basilea took a different approach. At that time she had not heard of organic farming. All she knew was that using poison is not the way to combat pests — not at Kanaan!

However, we were not so easily convinced. Our common sense told us, 'If everyone uses pesticides and we don't, then our grounds will be invaded by pests.' Eventually our attitude changed, as we came to see that, in God's eyes, there is a connection between pests and our sin. The fight against pests was necessary not only for practical purposes but for spiritual reasons: no canker-worm of sin was to be tolerated in this land in which God had invested so much, otherwise all would be destroyed from within. The most destructive 'pests' are those entrenched in our hearts or seeking to invade them: self-righteousness, resentment, unwillingness to forgive, etc.

In this battle everything depended on actively tackling the 'pests' inside the heart as well as those out in the grounds. Then we experienced the truth of God's promise:

'I will rebuke the devourer for you, so that it will not destroy the fruits of your soil; and your vine in the field shall not fail to bear' (Malachi 3:11).

27

## The Joy of Dependence

Since time immemorial people have tried to control the weather. What a good thing we can't! Here, too, we are reminded of our dependence upon God.

Heavy rain clouds are hanging over Kanaan. The land is parched. It is raining in Darmstadt, it is raining in Eberstadt, but not on us. On another occasion what a surprise it is to return from Darmstadt or Eberstadt, where it has been dry, to discover that at Kanaan it has rained!

It is a literal fulfilment of the scripture: 'I also withheld the rain from you … I would send rain upon one city, and send no rain upon another city; one field would be rained upon, and the field on which it did not rain withered' (Amos 4:7).

This dependence upon God gives a great sense of security. At the mercy of neither people nor the forces of nature, we rest in the hands of our heavenly Father.

Looking back on the last 50 years, we can testify as Sisters of Mary that we have come to know and love the Father as He has raised and disciplined us as His children. Above all, we have come to know His infinite mercy, always far greater than our sins; even to the smallest signs of contrition and repentance He has responded with His abundant blessings.

No one has ever seen or heard of a God like you, who does such deeds for those who put their hope in him.

Isaiah 64:4 GNB

Lord, your constant
love reaches the heavens...
Your righteousness is
towering like the mountains...
How precious, O God,
is your constant love!
We find protection under
the shadow of your wings.
We feast on the abundant
food you provide;
you let us drink from the
river of your goodness.

Psalm 36:5-8 GNB

# FATHER OF GOODNESS

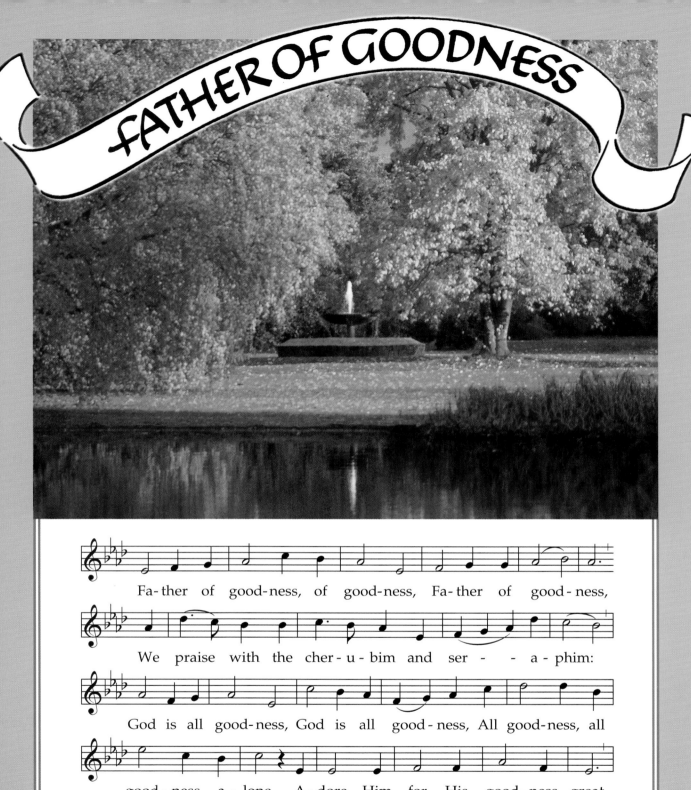

Fa-ther of good-ness, of good-ness, Fa-ther of good-ness,

We praise with the cher-u-bim and ser - - a-phim:

God is all good-ness, God is all good-ness, All good-ness, all

good-ness a - lone. A-dore Him for His good-ness great.

Yes, God is goodness, Yes, God is goodness, goodness a-lone.

Fa-ther of goodness, of goodness, Fa-ther of good-ness.

Erbaut allein
durch die Hilfe des
Herrn, der Himmel
und Erde
gemacht hat,

im GLAUBEN an
JESUS
CHRISTUS

2  3

32

# Built Alone
# with the Help of the Lord

Prayer and worship was the first ministry entrusted to our sisterhood by God. He impressed upon the hearts of our spiritual mothers that this was to be the essence of our life and the mainspring of all other ministries. It could not be otherwise, since those who love God have the desire to bring Him praise, glory and worship. Today, in an age of widespread blasphemy, this is especially relevant.

In May 1949 Mother Basilea was inwardly directed to build a chapel for the Lord Jesus, where He would receive adoration. With Steinberg House bursting at the seams, no new sisters could join, so a Mother House had also to be built.

All we had was 30 Marks. But our financial backer was the Lord — as even the building authorities came to accept! 'Our help is in the name of the Lord, who made heaven and earth' (Psalm 124:8) was the scripture He had given us.

To this day visitors arriving at the Mother House are greeted by a banner proclaiming, 'Built alone with the help of the Lord, who made heaven and earth — by faith in Jesus Christ'. Our Mother House Chapel is a testimony to the Lord whose name is Yes and Amen and who can create something new out of ruins, for this building was literally made with bricks salvaged from the ruins of our city.

*Realities* tells the story. How encouraging to know that this book inspired others in various parts of the world to build in faith their own churches and halls — to the glory of God! The spiritual laws learnt during the building period hold good: persevering against overwhelming odds, renewed acts of dedication, humbling oneself and being reconciled. Who could have guessed that God would use our testimony to strengthen others launching out in faith? Every experience of a child of God has a purpose. What is hidden is meant to be revealed for the benefit of others (Mark 4:22). No one should underestimate the value of private daily struggles and troubles.

But the Mother House and Chapel were only the beginning. More building projects were to follow, keeping pace with a growing ministry.

1 *Mother House and Chapel, 1953*
2 *Banner at the entrance to the Mother House — initial capital for building*
3 *Mother Martyria with sisters salvaging bricks from the ruins*
4 *Construction of the Mother House*
5 *Dump cart*

4  5

'Let them make me a sanctuary, that I m[ay] dwell in their midst' (Exodus 25:8). This was t[he] scripture the Lord gave Mother Basilea [in] 1949 to confirm the building of the Moth[er] House Chapel. With the Lord's help, t[he] walls were raised in a short space of ti[me] and, on Good Friday 1951, a Lenten servi[ce] was held in the still unfinished buildir[g.] Dedicated as the Chapel of Jesus' Suffering[s,] it has become the heart of our sisterhood.

In a daily prayer service at 3 p.m., the ho[ur] of Jesus' death, we continue to rememb[er]

# The Chapel of Jesus' Sufferings

...e sufferings of Jesus as we accompany Him in spirit from Geth-
...mane to Calvary. Calvary is the place of renewal: there the
...ansformation of our lives begins through Jesus' redemptive sac-
...fice; there our hearts are rekindled with love and gratitude to
...im, as expressed in the words of Mother Martyria at the end of
...hree O'Clock Prayer:

> *In thanksgiving for Your redemption,*
> *we give ourselves to You in love.*
> *Graciously accept our offering*
> *that You may be loved more dearly*
> *and that our love*
> *may bring joy to Your heart. Amen.*

# Why a Second Chapel?

'May there be many loving You dearly,
Shining like suns with the radiance of love …'

From the Herald Chapel the call to love Jesus with 'first love' was to resound far and wide, awakening a response in many hearts. Our Lord was to receive glory and honour to make up for all the degradation He suffers today.

Spiritually, we found ourselves again on a dark avenue of faith with this building project. Everyone sees the need for building a school, a clinic or nursing home. But wouldn't a second chapel be considered an extravagance? How different is Jesus' verdict. He calls such *extravagance* 'a fine and beautiful thing for me' (Mark 14:6 GNB).

Finance wasn't the only problem. At that time our Herald Plays on biblical themes were not attracting large audiences. The few visitors hardly filled the small Mother House Chapel. And now a large building with a seating capacity of almost a thousand! Wouldn't the seats remain empty? Would people come?

*1-2 Herald Chapel, 1960*
*3   Herald Chapel interior, 1960s*
*4   Scene from a Herald Play*

Yet come they did! Over the years thousands have attended the worship services, Herald Plays, and celebrations. Together we have tasted the holy presence of the Lord while worshipping the Lamb and joyfully proclaiming Jesus' victory over the forces of evil.

1   Easter celebration
2,4 Festival at Kanaan
3   Our Dutch Kanaan minister from 1969 to 1979
5   Herald Chapel, chancel

# New Challenges of Faith

All further building projects at Kanaan pale before the Herald Chapel. Yet with rising costs and wages, we were faced with overwhelming odds each time.

Our most recent building, 'Jesus' Glory', a long-overdue and much-needed extension of the Mother House for our growing family of sisters, was a major challenge.

For years now we sisters have not been actively involved in building, and so our main contribution was prayer — trust mingled with apprehension in view of these new testings of faith rising like the builders' piles of sand to dizzying heights before our eyes.

*Below right:
discussion with our architect*

41

It is well-known that, when the builders leave, the bills arrive. But the bills were unexpectedly high because of the difficulties of joining the new building to the Mother House and the necessary renovation of parts of the old building.

In order not to stand in God's way, we need to ask ourselves in His light whether or not we are good stewards of His gifts. Only those who are faithful in little things will be entrusted by God with greater things (Matthew 25:14–30).

In His goodness God over and over again graciously intervened by sending help, often at the very last moment. As with all our building

42

rojects, we can testify that every bill was paid on time without us ever having to take out a loan or mortgage.

rom oldest to youngest, we were thankful for this latest opportunity to exercise faith, tested to the limits though was. Mother Basilea spelt out the implications for us:

OLLOWING PATHS OF FAITH ENTAILS SUFFERING. Paths of ith teach us to tread carefully as far as our sin is conerned and to seek the will of God constantly. Yet these ame paths also acquaint us with the heart of God, who elights in showing us goodness. Ventures of faith bring glory to the name of God; and because faith makes us dependent upon the Father, we become more deeply united with Him on such pathways...

When we look ahead, how encouraging it is to know that God never changes. At the beginning of our sisterhood, when we had absolutely nothing, we appealed to Him as the God who does marvellous things. From 1947 to this very day, He has lived up to His name, being to us

## for 50 years a Father of goodness!

1 Longtime Canaan Friend and carpenter, who assisted in building the Mother House, now working on the extension
2 Construction supervisors well-pleased with progress
3 Our electrician
4 Renovation of the old building
5-8 Dedication of the extension, June 11, 1994: kitchen — building contractor's family — extension viewed from the woods — viewed from the street

8

6

7

# *I will rejoice in doing them good.* Jeremiah 32:41

Our mothers became increasingly convinced that living by faith was to be extended to trusting God for our daily bread, so that we would learn to be completely dependent on the goodness of our heavenly Father. It was an unusual leading, perhaps too impractical for some. 'At the moment it might work, but just wait till there are a hundred of you!' went the argument. However, in Mother Basilea's heart the longing persisted:

'We want to bring joy to the Father by trusting solely in His fatherly love to care and provide for His children. And it is our prayer that we will consequently draw all the closer to Him, responding with much thanksgiving, praise and love for His help and miraculous intervention…'

Such a desire stands in stark contrast to the pursuit of material gain and financial security characterizing society today. Yet while some seek greater wealth, others struggle to survive economically. In times like these it is vital that God's children trust implicitly in the Father's goodness and provision. Then His power and love will be demonstrated, as a testimony to others. Holy Scripture, however, does state preconditions: 'Seek first his kingdom and his righteousness, and all these things shall be yours as well' (Matthew 6:33).

In view of the greed and selfishness deeply rooted in human nature, repentance and faith are essential. Meeting the conditions of Matthew 6:33 is always a spiritual struggle. But when the Lord does have first place again in our lives, we experience the truth of the mosaic in the Mother House entrance —'…and yet your heavenly Father feeds them' (Matthew 6:26).

This has been our experience all these years, whether stationed overseas in twos or cooking like our kitchen sisters at Kanaan for approximately 200 daily. Each one of us could relate how lovingly and personally the Father has provided — sometimes in highly original ways.

*Oh, trust His goodness,*
*trust His faithfulness.*
*He will never forsake you.*
*His mercies*
*are new every morning.*

# 50
## OF FA
## GOO

ARS
ERLY
ESS

For God
so loved
the world that
he gave his
only begotten Son,
that whoever
believes in him
should not perish
but have
everlasting life.

John 3:16 RAV

# FATHER OF LOVE

Lov - ing Fa - ther, lov - ing Fa - ther, Fa - ther of

ev - er - last - ing love, My heart sings with joy of

Your un - end - ing love, Your plan - ning, lead - ing, coun - sel.

Lov - ing Fa - ther, lov - ing Fa - ther, Fa - ther of

ev - er - last - ing love, All - lov - ing You are!

> *If Christ were born a thousand times in Bethlehem but not in you, you would be eternally lost.*
>
> Angelus Silesius (1624-1677)

For us, as Sisters of Mary, Christmas 1952 was an unforgettable occasion. Until then the mystery of Christmas had been, largely, something abstract for us — mere knowledge, tradition, rather than living reality.

Now God wanted to do a new thing among us: we were to learn the secret of spiritual childlikeness in keeping with Matthew 18:3.

Convinced of this, Mother Basilea held on in faith even though no change was evident on Christmas Eve, only a stifling weariness and heaviness in the atmosphere. For weeks she had lived in expectation of Christmas, composing many songs in adoration of the Child Jesus. On December 26, the breakthrough came:

> *O Child, You make us childlike,*
> *Much loved and showing love,*
> *Our whole lives to You giving,*
> *Who came from heav'n above.*

Never before had we experienced such a worshipful atmosphere as we praised and adored God for what He had given us in this Child: forgiveness of sin, joy, love for one another — a foretaste of heaven. 'For God so loved the world that he gave his only begotten Son…' (RAV). These words took on a new significance for us. It was like reliving the first Christmas.

Years later this experience recurs Christmas after Christmas in other places, at home and abroad, including the Nativity Grotto in Bethlehem. Like rays of light filtering into every corner, the joyous celebration finds its way to schools and prisons, hospitals and nursing homes, shopping malls and market-

squares—even television. Love Divine in the form of a little Child continues to touch hearts and transform lives …

'It all began that Christmas when you sisters came with Baby Jesus in a bamboo crib to the tiny living space allotted to me and my daughters,' related a Buddhist Vietnamese at a refugee camp in Hong Kong. 'In my homeland, when passing by the beautifully decorated churches at Christmas time, I would often look inside with a longing heart. But I always went away feeling it wasn't for me because I wasn't good enough. Then as I saw the crib in our hovel, I suddenly understood that He had come to *me* …'

1   *Bethlehem in the Holy Land*

2   *Bethlehem Grotto at Kanaan*

3   *Carol-singing on Christmas Eve,*
    *Nativity Grotto, Bethlehem*

4   *Greece*

5-6 *England*

7   *Carol-singing*

8   *Hospital ward, Zambia*

# The Garden of Jesus' Sufferings

Nowhere does the love of God come so close to us as in the sufferings of His Son. This is why at Kanaan there is a place helping us visualize the Passion of Christ. In the life of Count Zinzendorf, the great reformer, the turning point came as he was contemplating a painting of Christ wearing the crown of thorns. Its inscription read, 'All this I did for you. What are you doing for Me?' This question stands invisibly over the Garden of Jesus' Sufferings.

'When Jesus is portrayed as the Man of Sorrows, this is no figure of speech. It is reality. Here is Someone who actually suffered, endured and emerged as victor over sin and grief. Here we encounter the fairest of the sons of men, who in the midst of immeasurable suffering, humiliation, disappointments and insults, radiated love. His love is the supreme power, which can help us all in every plight and kindle us with love for God and our fellow beings.'

Taken from: *Where Can We Find Jesus?*

In the mid 1960s, when the Garden of Jesus' Sufferings at Kanaan was designed with works of art, we little dreamt that one day similar prayer gardens would be established in other parts of the world. For many, God has made these gardens a place where He reveals His love — though often using unusual ways of drawing people's attention to them …

For instance, on the eve of Palm Sunday 1994, a television news announcer in Phoenix, Arizona, said: 'Each year thousands of Christians travel to the Holy Land to retrace Christ's steps during His last days. You may not have to travel those thousands of miles to make that pilgrimage … [There's] a special place right here in Arizona where you can experience Christ's Passion …' Recommended in the Visitor's Guide as one of the attractions of the Phoenix area, the garden has an almost constant flow of visitors daily.

*1-2 Garden of Jesus' Sufferings at Kanaan, 1964-1965*
*3-5 Canada*

56

3

4

5

1 Norway    2-3 Canada
4 Kanaan    5-6 USA

5

6

*Is* it nothing to you,
    all you who pass by?
Look and see if there is
    any sorrow like my sorrow.

Lamentations 1:12

The Passion of Christ began with three sleeping disciples. Sleeping … Could the same be said of us today? For us, too, the clarion call is: 'Watch and pray' (Matthew 26:41).

'We are exposed to unprecedented attacks by the powers of darkness. The danger of being sucked into deception and lawlessness is very real. The atmosphere is oppressive, generating fear and depression … Therefore, we are challenged, as never before, to pray and engage in spiritual warfare, proclaiming, "Jesus is Victor! Jesus is Victor!" We cannot pray these words often enough. They have power whether we pray them silently or aloud. Then the forces of darkness that sought to ensnare us will yield …

'At the same time we are challenged to pray as Jesus did in Gethsemane. His was a very special prayer, a prayer of tremendous power that drove Satan away, a prayer expressive of deepest adoration: "My Father … not as I will, but as thou wilt" (Matthew 26:39). The prayer "Yes, Father" cost Jesus the deepest agony of soul. It was an unconditional surrender to the greatest suffering of all.'

Taken from: *Strong in the Time of Testing*

As Christians we can be adept at talking about faith in Jesus without actually following Him in practice — a ploy of Satan. There is a difference between mere words and discipleship. Jesus challenges us to take up our cross daily and follow Him.

Called to follow His example of humility and obedience, we are to walk in His footsteps (Philippians 2:5-8; 1 Peter 2:21). It is in the discipleship of the cross that we truly enter into the fellowship of love with Him.

*Entrance to the Garden of Jesus' Sufferings, Australia*

*The Stone Pavement (John 19:13), Garden of Jesus' Sufferings, Kanaan*

**61**

1

2

3

*Garden of Jesus' Sufferings:*
*1 Australia   2 Paraguay   3,4 Norway*

Throughout His Passion Jesus did not receive a single word of comfort or sign of love from His disciples. On the contrary, they forsook and denied Him … Love for Him did not spring up until, humanly speaking, it was too late. When it did come, it was the precious fruit of His suffering and finished work of redemption on the cross.

After so much failure, now for the first time someone was prepared to risk his life by identifying with Jesus: Joseph of Arimathea dared to approach the Roman governor, Pilate, in order to show Jesus a last act of respect in preparing a worthy burial place for His body. Now there was a willingness to show Him love, to sacrifice and suffer on His behalf, without the Lord being able to respond by word or glance. This was the birth of consoling love, a love free from mixed motives, a selfless love, seeking Him alone.

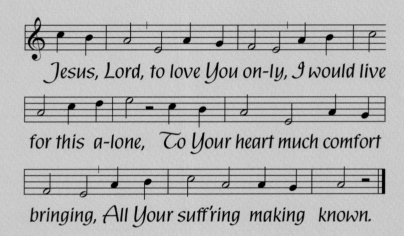

Jesus, Lord, to love You on-ly, I would live
for this a-lone, To Your heart much comfort
bringing, All Your suff'ring making known.

Naught I care now for my troubles,
Since I've seen Your pain and grief;
I would live now to console You,
Would bear suff'ring willingly.

May my heart now burn within me
For Your grief and agony.
Oh, that souls would heed Your suff'ring
And Your comforters then be!

*Garden of Jesus' Sufferings, Taiwan*

The Lord is risen! He is risen indeed a

'n our midst as all-conquering love! ✦

*Garden of Jesus'*
*Sufferings,*
*Phoenix,*
*Arizona (USA)*

## Holy Land,

*that I may walk here! Step by step my Lord and Saviour
tells me of His life and way, draws me with Him every day.*

*Holy Land,
with joy I'm singing, all my worship to Him bringing.
Here He wrought such wondrous deeds,
healed the blind, supplied all needs.*

*Holy Land,
beside my Saviour I would stand in grief and sorrow,
live for Him who for me died, that He may be glorified
at these sites when He returns.*

'Put off your shoes from your feet, for the place
on which you are standing is holy ground.'

Exodus 3:5

How fitting is this scripture for those places in
Israel associated with God's redemptive purposes. There His beloved Son lived, suffered — and
sacrificed Himself for us. There, too, He rose from
the dead and ascended to heaven. And there He
will come again at the close of the age as Lord
and King.

In Mother Basilea's heart a fire was kindled: If
only we could help prepare these places for His
return — in response to His love and suffering.
What joy for Him when lives are touched and
transformed through encountering His love at
these sites! Tourists become pilgrims.

For over 30 years now our Holy Land plaques
and the pamphlet *The Holy Places Today* have con-
tributed to this end. A larger book for pilgrims,
*The Holy Land Today*, is used even by Israeli
guides. Unthinkable previously, we were asked
to design and produce bas-reliefs for historical
sites to help make the events of long ago come
alive.

**5**

O MY FATHER,
IF IT BE POSSIBLE, LET THIS CUP PASS FROM ME;
NEVERTHELESS NOT MY WILL, BUT YOURS BE DONE.

Matthew 26/39

You, o Jesus, in Gethsemane,
in deepest night and agony,
spoke these words of surrender
and trust to God the Father.
In gratitude and love I want to say with You
in my hours of fear and trouble:

My Father,
I do not understand You, but I trust You.

MB

MEIN VATER,
WENN ES MÖGLICH IST, SO LASS DIESEN KELCH
AN MIR VORÜBERGEHEN. DOCH NICHT WIE ICH
WILL, SONDERN WIE DU WILLST.    Matthäus 26/39

Du, o Jesus, hast in Gethsemane
in tiefster Nacht und Qual
dies Wort der Hingabe und des Vertrauens
zu Gott-Vater gesprochen.
Aus Dank und Liebe will ich mit Dir sprechen
in Stunden meiner Angst und Not:

Mein Vater,
ich verstehe Dich nicht, aber ich vertraue Dir.

MB

1  *Bethesda*

2  *Bethlehem*

3  *Bas-relief, Garden of Gethsemane*

4  *Bethany*

5  *Plaque, Garden of Gethsemane*

6  *The Holy Steps,
   bas-reliefs commemorating night of Jesus' arrest*

In Jerusalem, on the Via Dolorosa, a tourist discovered one of our plaques and was deeply convicted. Not long afterwards she spotted the next plaque and read it aloud, oblivious of her surroundings. Her companion was reluctant to linger. But she insisted, 'If something is written on the walls of Jerusalem, then it must be important and so I want to read it.' Soon they came across a third plaque, which she also read aloud. Deeply moved, she stood there a while.

And so it was each time.

When they arrived at Calvary, the lady gave her life to Jesus and went home a new person.

**God** has revealed his grace for the salvation of all mankind.

Titus 2 : 11 GNB

# FATHER OF GRACE

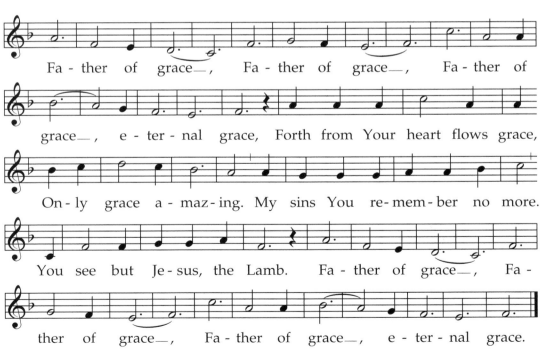

Fa - ther of grace—, Fa - ther of grace—, Fa - ther of grace—, e - ter - nal grace, Forth from Your heart flows grace, On - ly grace a - maz - ing. My sins You re - mem - ber no more. You see but Je - sus, the Lamb. Fa - ther of grace—, Fa - ther of grace—, Fa - ther of grace—, e - ter - nal grace.

Lord Jesus Christ,
Kindle in me a growing longing to come
to the foot of the cross,
of all places the most wonderful,
the place where a sinner is made righteous,
where You fold him in Your arms,
where heaven opens up for him,
and where You, Lord Jesus, assure him,
saying, 'Your sins are forgiven.
This day you will be with Me in paradise.'
Lord, bring me back again
to this place more often, the place
where Your heart seeks me. Amen.

This prayer captures something of our mothers' lifelong goal of faith for Kanaan and the Sisterhood of Mary: the dawning of paradise, the presence of God, among us. Paradise has an unshakeable foundation in Jesus' sacrificial death at Calvary.

The first to experience this personally was one of the two criminals crucified with Jesus. He recognized the innocence of Jesus as He hung there, subjected to mockery and torment; at the same time he acknowledged, in deep contrition, that he himself was receiving the just reward of his deeds. There was nothing he could do to make up for the past; yet, filled with trust, he turned to Jesus and heard Him utter those amazing words: 'Truly, I say to you, today you will be with me in Paradise' (Luke 23:43).

We need such a penitent attitude. 'For thus says the high and lofty One who inhabits eternity, whose name is Holy: "I dwell in the high and holy place, and also with him who is of a contrite and humble spirit, to revive the spirit of the humble, and to revive the heart of the contrite"' (Isaiah 57:15). Mother Martyria had the special gift of making the foot of the cross precious to us. When counselling us, she would say, for instance, 'God leads us away from success and victory — into defeat. He leads us along paths where we increasingly sense our helplessness. Then we have no option but to flee into the arms of Christ — not as self-pitying

hypocrites in hurt pride, but as genuinely contrite souls, convicted of our nothingness and desiring only Christ.' In this way the love of Jesus is poured out upon us — and we taste paradise.

This coming to the foot of the cross inevitably entails a spiritual struggle — no surprise to anyone who knows himself and the Bible. To help in this spiritual warfare, the Lord gave Mother Basilea numerous songs celebrating His victorious might. Translated into many languages, these have been tried and tested in proclaiming Jesus' victory in all kinds of situations: the personal struggle against sin; everyday difficulties; trials and temptations; praying against esoteric trends and occult forces.

'May we shout for joy over your victory, and in the name of our God set up our banners!' In keeping with these words from Psalm 20:5, we often use banners of faith inscribed with victory verses from the Bible when battling in faith. Such assurance of victory overcomes any sense of discouragement threatening to keep us from being happy in Jesus; in all our struggles we are filled with the joy of the Lord.

*Left: Garden of Jesus' Sufferings, Phoenix, Arizona (USA)*

Living in a large family offers many opportunities for practising reconciliation, forgiving one another and being forgiven. Comprising 19 nationalities, differing in background and training, sometimes coming straight from school, we live and work closely together. Given these circumstances, misunderstandings and irritations are not unexpected. But when everyone comes to the foot of the cross, joy prevails — be it among us, the Sisters of Mary, or the Sisters of the Crown of Thorns (women called later in life), or the Canaan Franciscan Brothers. 'Be reconciled. Don't be at odds with anyone …' These words from our Rule are just as binding

for our Sisters of Thorns and Canaan Friends, who seek to follow the Lord where He has placed them and, in addition to their obligations at home and work, are actively involved in our ministry. Jesus once impressed upon His disciples, 'The harvest is plentiful, but the labourers are few; pray therefore the Lord of the harvest to send out labourers into his harvest' (Matthew 9:37-38). These words are equally relevant today, for there remains much to be done in the Lord's vineyard. No one is superfluous; even those incapacitated by age or sickness can continue the main work — the hidden ministry of prayer.

If in the secular world productivity depends on good working relationships, this is even more true when it comes to serving the Lord. There is, in the Bible, a set of guidelines that is very effective, though radically at odds with the trend of our times.

'Don't do anything from selfish ambition or from a cheap desire to boast, but be humble towards one another, always considering others better than yourselves. And look out for one another's interests, not just for your own.'

Philippians 2:3-4 GNB

We try to live according to this principle and to be quick about removing the daily grit clogging the wheels. Our time and energy belongs to God and is too precious to waste on those little disagreements that spoil working relationships. In all our tasks we try to keep our eyes focused on the One we serve:

JESUS,
You are my one and all.
I want to talk with You
and work for You.
I want to think over everything
with You and make all my decisions
with You.
Nothing shall be done without You.
Bind me tightly to You,
so that I constantly live in Your
holy presence:
for You are there!

Taken from: 'My All for Him'

JESUS
keiner ist JHM gleich.

Darum ist ER zu lieben
wie sonst keiner,
mehr denn alle anderen,
mehr als alles andere.

JHN
ausschließlich
zu lieben,
bist du berufen.

4

Love for Jesus is the mainspring of everything at Kanaan and in the branches. 'This love is soundly rooted in repentance, which means seeing your sins, being sorry about them and making a clean break with them. This has been my experience and the experience of others. Genuine, pure, ardent love for Jesus grows out of contrition and the experience of His forgiveness, as Holy Scripture demonstrates in the story of the great sinner, who came to love her Saviour with a deep devotion (Luke 7:44-48). And this love is a divine gift of grace.'

Taken from: 'Bride of Jesus Christ'

From the Messages to the Seven Churches (Revelation 2-3) it is evident what Jesus' primary concern for believers is. The church at Ephesus, for instance, had much that was commendable. Yet Jesus called its activities and achievements into question, because 'first love' for Him had been abandoned. And Peter, who denied Jesus three times, was asked three times by the risen Lord not 'Do you believe in Me?' but,

### 'Do you love Me?'

Again and again this is the essential question Jesus asks all believers.

For love of the Lord some even remain unmarried in order to serve Him with more single-minded devotion. Jesus Himself recognizes this, saying, '…others do not marry for the sake of the Kingdom of heaven' (Matthew 19:12 GNB). In keeping with this calling to love Jesus above all else, life in the sisterhood is based on the discipleship of the cross, for it is in the nitty-gritty of everyday situations that love for the Lord is tested.

For us, as Sisters of Mary, the radiant joy of belonging to Jesus is perhaps most visible on the day of our bridal dedication, usually seven years after admission. In His Word He promises, 'He who loses his life for my sake will find

it' (Matthew 10:39). And *finding* means bliss and fulfilment even here and now.

Loving Jesus and being loved by Him is the purpose of our lives. But this does not stop with us as Sisters of Mary. Everyone (young and old, male and female, married and single) is called to love the Lord — and everyone is offered His love. Continuing even when human love comes to an end, His love and joy are beyond expression.

*O none can be loved as is Jesus.*
*None like Him is found anywhere.*
*'Tis He whom I love, whom I live for,*
*For no one with Him can compare.*

*So all that I have I will give Him,*
*I'll sacrifice all I hold dear.*
*My whole life to Jesus belonging,*
*My heart seeks my Lord to revere.*

*My heart is at peace and so joyful,*
*For all I desire He supplies.*
*I look now for nothing but Jesus,*
*Who all of my hopes satisfies.*

Taken from: 'O None Can Be Loved Like Jesus'

---

1   *Jesus Pathway, Kanaan. Text: 'No one can compare with Jesus, and so He is to be loved as none other, more than anyone else and more than anything else. This is your calling: to love Him exclusively.'*

2   *Altar cloth with the sisterhood's emblem*

3-4 *Sisters on the day of their bridal dedication*   79

*I*n the mid 1960s God showed there would be a fellowship of brothers with the same vocation serving at Kanaan in the spirit of first love for Jesus.

Just as the name 'Sisters of Mary' points to our spiritual goal of following Jesus to the cross after the example of Mary, His mother, so St. Francis of Assisi is in a special sense an example for the Canaan Franciscan Brothers. In the life of St. Francis something can be seen of the blessing of a man dedicated to God, inspiring Christians down through the centuries to the present day. How vividly Mother Basilea once shared with the brothers what St. Francis means to her:

'In his personality, conduct and life I encountered the heart of the Gospel: "Unless you become like little children…" By living out the Gospel message (which includes surrendering earthly goods, losing one's life, embracing poverty for body, soul and spirit), St. Francis was counted among the blessed according to the words of the Beatitudes, "Blessed are the poor…" And indeed, he was blessed, living in heaven even in this life. As the joyful troubadour he did not call others to follow paths of renunciation in an ascetic, legalistic way, but invited them to enter into the freedom of God's children, who are led by the Spirit of God. It was ardent love for Jesus, kindled by daily repentance, that constrained him to suffer and make sacrifices for the Lord who had suffered immeasurably for all of us.

'This captivating childlikeness and humility, the source of all power and authority in ministry for Jesus, touched my heart. Being more intellectually inclined by nature, I yearned deeply for this spirit to fill my own life. A burning love for Jesus, a close communion of the heart with Him who is the source of all joy — this I could see in the life of St. Francis. And it strengthened me in my desire to love Jesus more. From the effects of St. Francis' life and discipleship I realized that only fervent love for Jesus provides a solution to problems and difficulties in the Church and the world — as St. Francis demonstrated in his day.'

Today, 30 years later, we cannot thank God enough for His wisdom in calling brothers to play an active role in the ministry at Kanaan. Whether in the areas of farming, building maintenance, and transport, or in the film- and audio-departments, or in the realm of computers and telecommunications, they serve the Lord with dedication, regardless of the cost.

*Sculpture of St. Francis of Assisi
in the brothers' prayer garden*

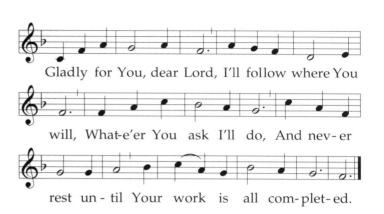

Gladly for You, dear Lord, I'll follow where You will, What-e'er You ask I'll do, And nev-er rest un-til Your work is all com-plet-ed.

Gladly for You, dear Lord, and for Your honour's sake,
all that You ask I'll do, Your greater glory make
the aim of all my living.

Gladly for You, dear Lord, whate'er the cost may be,
my heart and will I give, for You are all to me.
I give You all I treasure.

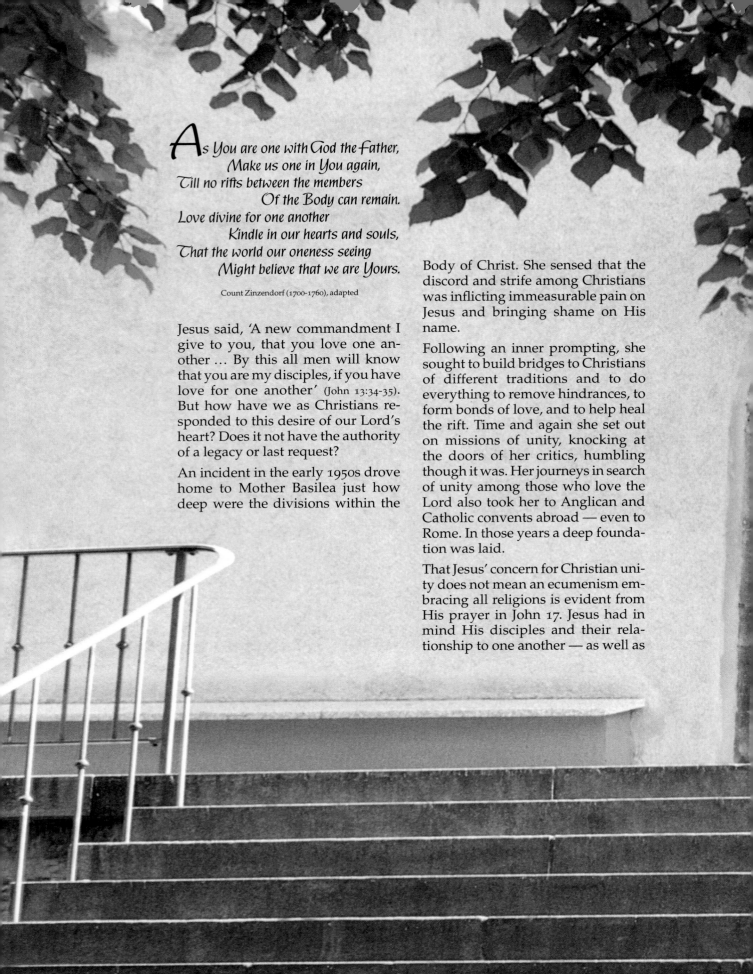

*As You are one with God the Father,*
*Make us one in You again,*
*Till no rifts between the members*
*Of the Body can remain.*
*Love divine for one another*
*Kindle in our hearts and souls,*
*That the world our oneness seeing*
*Might believe that we are Yours.*

Count Zinzendorf (1700-1760), adapted

Jesus said, 'A new commandment I give to you, that you love one another … By this all men will know that you are my disciples, if you have love for one another' (John 13:34-35). But how have we as Christians responded to this desire of our Lord's heart? Does it not have the authority of a legacy or last request?

An incident in the early 1950s drove home to Mother Basilea just how deep were the divisions within the Body of Christ. She sensed that the discord and strife among Christians was inflicting immeasurable pain on Jesus and bringing shame on His name.

Following an inner prompting, she sought to build bridges to Christians of different traditions and to do everything to remove hindrances, to form bonds of love, and to help heal the rift. Time and again she set out on missions of unity, knocking at the doors of her critics, humbling though it was. Her journeys in search of unity among those who love the Lord also took her to Anglican and Catholic convents abroad — even to Rome. In those years a deep foundation was laid.

That Jesus' concern for Christian unity does not mean an ecumenism embracing all religions is evident from His prayer in John 17. Jesus had in mind His disciples and their relationship to one another — as well as

82

all future believers. Today, as then, He is concerned about His followers being one in love.

Recent years have seen a real breakthrough among those who love the Lord. Across denominational and national barriers, bonds of fellowship have been forged, for

*The closer we are*
    *to the loving heart of God,*
*the closer we are to one another.*

*...that they may all be one.*

John 17:21

He who touches you
touches th...

ALSFELD אלספלד
GREBENAU גרעבנאו
LAUTERBACH
ANGENROD אנגנרוד
ULRICHSTEIN אולריכשטיין
NIEDER-OHMEN נידער-אומן
CRAINFELD קריינפעלד
GIESSEN גיסן
HUNGEN BUTZBACH הונגן בוצבא
ALLENDORF אלנדורף
DÜDELSHEIM דידלסהיים
GEDERN גדרן
SCHOTTEN שוטן
LICH ליך
OBERSEEMEN
FRIEDBERG פרידברג
BAD NAUHEIM באד נאוהיים
REICHELSHEIM רייכלסהיים
GROSS-KARBEN גרוס-קארבן
BÜDINGEN בידינגן
GAMBACH גאמבאך
RODHEIM רודהיים
ECHZELL
BAD VILBEL באד פילבל
ALTENSTADT אלטנשטאט
BÜDESHEIM
NIDDA נידה
HELDENBERGEN הלדנברגן
OFFENBACH אופנבאך
BÜRGEL בירגל
LANGEN לאנגן
MÜHLHEIM מילהיים
SPRENDLINGEN שפרנדלינגן
MAINZ מגנצא
NEU-ISENBURG נוי-איזנבורג
SELIGENSTADT זעליגנשטאט
EGELSBACH אגלסבאך
GROSS-UMSTADT גרוס-אומשטאט
DIEBURG דיבורג
OPPENHEIM אופנהיים
GROSS-GERAU גרוס-גראו
PFUNGSTADT פפונגשטאט
DARMSTADT דארמשטאט
GRIESHEIM גריסהיים
BABENHAUSEN באבנהאוזן
EBERSTADT אברשטאט
GROSS-ZIMMERN גרוס-צימרן
OBER-RAMSTADT אובר-ראמשטאט
FÜRFELD פירפלד
ALZEY אלציי
FLONHEIM פלונהיים
WORMS וורמייזא
OSTHOFEN אוסטהופן
GUNTERSBLUM גונטרסבלום

1

*Without end the blood on our hands cries out to heaven: the serious crime against Israel. Immeasurably high and beyond all telling is the mountain of our guilt.*

*Let us repent deeply, humbling ourselves in the dust before those whom we have cruelly driven to their deaths. Oh, that we would now seek to make amends for the evil we have done, showing kindness to the people of God!*

*May Jesus, the Lamb of God, by whose wounds we are healed, be ever before us. He is the one we have afflicted. Oh, listen to His lament, 'Your blows against My people have fallen on Me.'* Taken from: 'Prayer for Israel'

As Germans, we can only humble ourselves beneath this guilt and, in the spirit of Daniel 9, confess, 'I and my people have sinned.' Here, too, our mothers set us an example — even though in the Third Reich they had taken a clear stand against Hitler. As National President of the Women's Division of the German Student Christian Movement, Mother Basilea rejected Nazi policy, e.g. the introduction of the Aryan Paragraph, which would have debarred Jewish Christians from the movement. In view of the countless atrocities committed in the name of the German people, which generation we belong to or whether we are personally implicated or not is irrelevant. We unite in confessing:

We have failed to love God's chosen people. We have sinned grievously against them. We must share the blame for the death of millions of Jews, having done little or nothing to rescue them. We, the Christian community in general, were like the priest and Levite in Luke 10, who cold-heartedly passed by the man attacked by robbers and left to die. We looked the other way. We were silent, failing the Jews in the hour of their greatest need. Our personal safety meant more to us than the commandment to show love and compassion.

*Have mercy on me, O God, according to thy steadfast love; according to thy abundant mercy blot out my transgressions. Wash me thoroughly from my iniquity, and cleanse me from my sin! For I know my transgressions, and my sin is ever before me.* Psalm 51:1-3

1 Names of lost Jewish communities at Holocaust memorial Yad Vashem, Jerusalem
2-3 Memorial site of former concentration camp Dachau, Germany — plaque of penitence, Church of Reconciliation

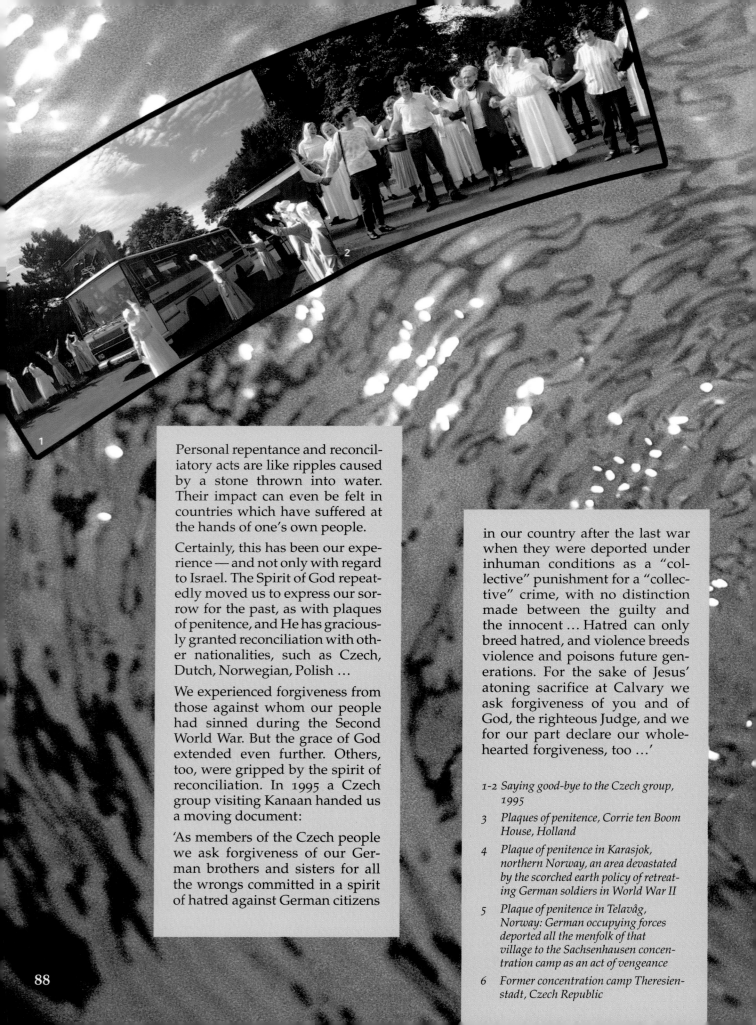

Personal repentance and reconciliatory acts are like ripples caused by a stone thrown into water. Their impact can even be felt in countries which have suffered at the hands of one's own people.

Certainly, this has been our experience — and not only with regard to Israel. The Spirit of God repeatedly moved us to express our sorrow for the past, as with plaques of penitence, and He has graciously granted reconciliation with other nationalities, such as Czech, Dutch, Norwegian, Polish …

We experienced forgiveness from those against whom our people had sinned during the Second World War. But the grace of God extended even further. Others, too, were gripped by the spirit of reconciliation. In 1995 a Czech group visiting Kanaan handed us a moving document:

'As members of the Czech people we ask forgiveness of our German brothers and sisters for all the wrongs committed in a spirit of hatred against German citizens in our country after the last war when they were deported under inhuman conditions as a "collective" punishment for a "collective" crime, with no distinction made between the guilty and the innocent … Hatred can only breed hatred, and violence breeds violence and poisons future generations. For the sake of Jesus' atoning sacrifice at Calvary we ask forgiveness of you and of God, the righteous Judge, and we for our part declare our wholehearted forgiveness, too …'

1-2 Saying good-bye to the Czech group, 1995

3 Plaques of penitence, Corrie ten Boom House, Holland

4 Plaque of penitence in Karasjok, northern Norway, an area devastated by the scorched earth policy of retreating German soldiers in World War II

5 Plaque of penitence in Telavåg, Norway: German occupying forces deported all the menfolk of that village to the Sachsenhausen concentration camp as an act of vengeance

6 Former concentration camp Theresienstadt, Czech Republic

88

# RECONCILIATION IS CONTAGIOUS

'A history of 200 years of injustice and guilt stands between the indigenous people — the Aborigines — and us Whites,' write our sisters in Australia. 'So how touched we were when a group of Aborigine Christians wanted to come to us at all, travelling over 3000 kilometres to attend a retreat at our branch near Sydney. As Whites we could only humble ourselves before them. When Canaan Friends, descendants of the first settlers, asked their forgiveness on behalf of White Australians, it was like the sun breaking through the clouds…'

Since 1969 sectarian violence has dominated life in Northern Ireland. Our sisters report: 'Prior to a meeting in a Belfast suburb, Catholic nuns told us that a militant Protestant group had just wreaked havoc in their church. Even so, many Protestants came that evening to the Catholic church hall. After our confession, as Germans, of national guilt during the war, everyone present got down on their knees. The Protestants humbled themselves before their Catholic brothers and sisters with tears and asked for their forgiveness. The Catholics responded by saying, "We have also committed many wrongs against you." Kneeling, we prayed together the words of Psalm 51, each according to his version. There was such a move of repentance, mutual forgiveness and love that it was one-and-a-half hours before we could show our film.'

Where there is repentance and a willingness to be reconciled, wounds begin to heal. Time and again this has happened in encounters between Whites and North

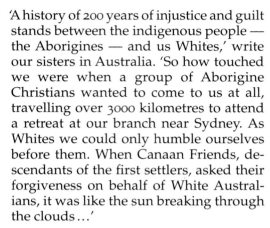

American Indians, Whites and New Zealand Maoris, Japanese and Koreans…

One of our videos on this theme (*Christmas — A Time to Forgive*) is being used by God to help sow reconciliation in multiracial societies as, for instance, in the Americas and Africa … The Russian version was even televised in Volgograd, formerly Stalingrad. During World War II hundreds of thousands of Russians and Germans lost their lives in the battle for this city, an event known in history as 'the hell of Stalingrad'. Only recently has the process of reconciliation begun.

Asking for forgiveness can release something in another person's heart. Yet how many people worldwide wait in vain for such a request? What a tremendous opportunity God has given us! Not only may we ask for forgiveness, but by the grace of His forgiveness we can forgive others, thus breaking the vicious circle of hatred and bitterness.

1   *Ringing the bell, Chapel of Reconciliation, Australian branch*

2   *First contact with Aborigines, Elcho Island, Australia, 1984*

3   *Aborigines at the Australian branch, 1986*

4   *Prayer Garden 'God's Resting Place', Elcho Island*

5-6 *Northern Ireland*

7   *Garden of Jesus' Sufferings, Brazil*

The Lord
is not slow
to do what he
has promised,
as some think.
Instead, he is
patient with you,
because he
does not want
anyone to be
destroyed, but
wants all to
turn away
from their sins.

2 Peter 3:9 GNB

# FATHER OF PATIENCE

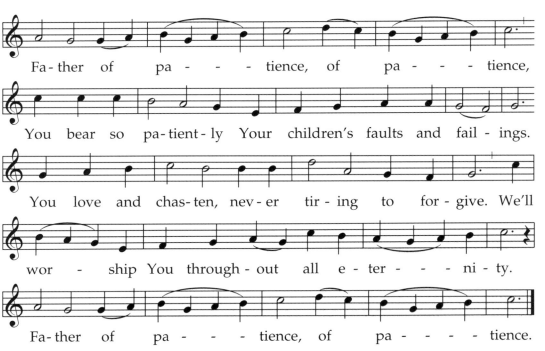

Fa- ther of pa - - tience, of pa - - tience,

You bear so pa- tient- ly Your children's faults and fail - ings.

You love and chas- ten, nev- er tir- ing to for- give. We'll

wor - ship You through- out all e- ter - - ni- ty.

Fa- ther of pa - - tience, of pa - - tience.

# LORD,

how long will You wait until You establish
Your rule?
Has the moment not yet come?
Two thousand years have elapsed.
O Lord, how humble You are!
You empty Yourself of Your power,
allowing people to mock and despise You
as once long ago
when You walked the earth.
Lord, is it not yet time to establish Your rule?

Today your Saviour Jesus Christ
is pleading with you in love.
God is pleading: Come back, come home.
The last hour is at hand.
Time is running out.

Excerpt from a Herald Play

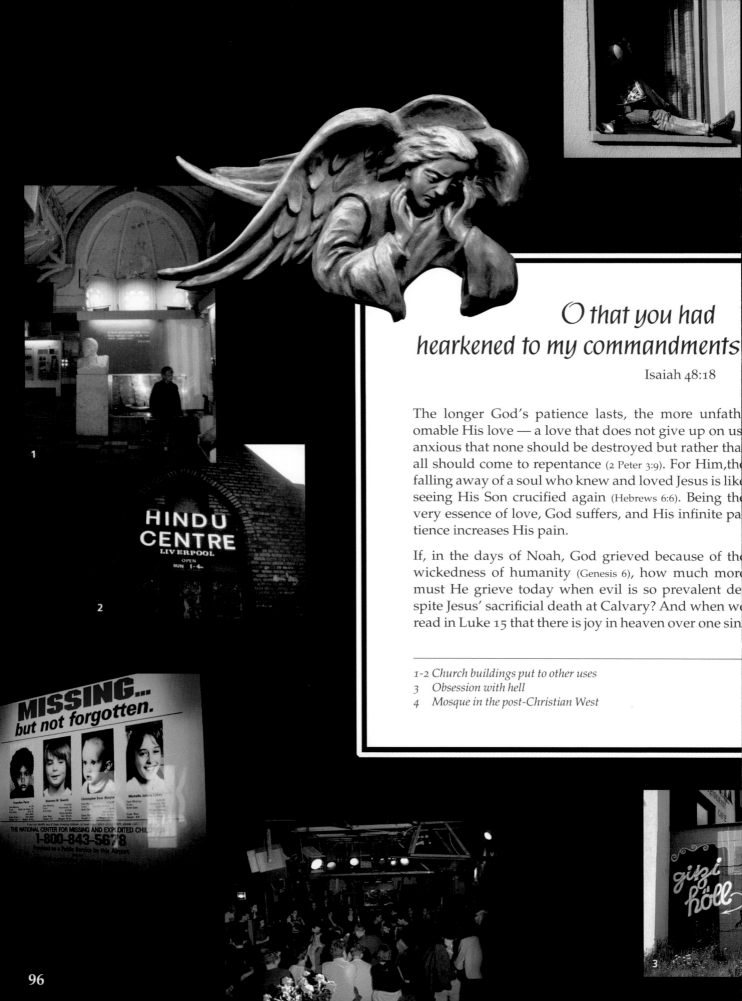

O *that you had*
*hearkened to my commandments*

Isaiah 48:18

The longer God's patience lasts, the more unfath
omable His love — a love that does not give up on us,
anxious that none should be destroyed but rather tha
all should come to repentance (2 Peter 3:9). For Him, the
falling away of a soul who knew and loved Jesus is like
seeing His Son crucified again (Hebrews 6:6). Being the
very essence of love, God suffers, and His infinite pa
tience increases His pain.

If, in the days of Noah, God grieved because of the
wickedness of humanity (Genesis 6), how much more
must He grieve today when evil is so prevalent de
spite Jesus' sacrificial death at Calvary? And when we
read in Luke 15 that there is joy in heaven over one sin

---

1-2 *Church buildings put to other uses*
3 *Obsession with hell*
4 *Mosque in the post-Christian West*

...her who repents, what weeping and mourning must
...ill heaven for all those who do not repent but delib-
...erately choose evil and so become a captive of hell?
...f only we could hear the words of Psalm 69 as if the
...Lord were speaking to us personally: 'I had hoped for
...sympathy, but there was none; for comfort, but I found
...none' (GNB).

Our Father's heart mourns ceaselessly
In deepest grief and agony,
So distant are His children.
In humble love He calls and pleads,
'My child, come home,' but who will heed?
Alone is He, forsaken.

He waits, though endless years have passed,
He knows He'll reach His goal at last,
His purposes accomplished:
His erring child back home again,
No more estranged and causing pain
But one with Him for ever.

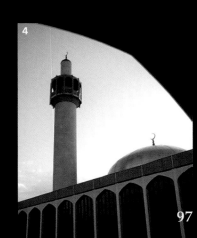

By walking in obedience to the commandments of God, you cannot go astray,
for you will be held fast and guided by the very will of God.

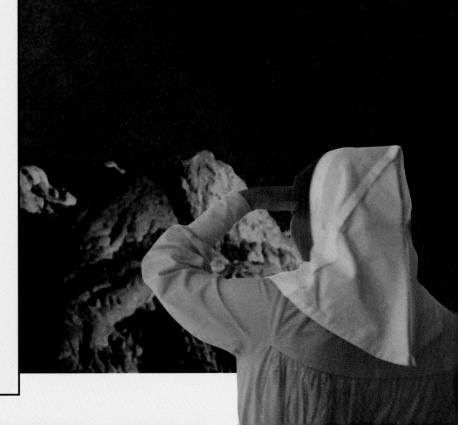

## Sinai – Mountain of God's Commandments

A stay at Mount Sinai, in autumn 1963, made a deep impact on Mother Basilea. The holy Ten Commandments, though so familiar to her, took on a new and deeper significance as a revelation of God's *loving* will. This was to influence the rest of her life and work — and thus our sisterhood.

Also in 1963 a bishop popularized radical theories that were previously almost unknown except among theologians. His view that 'the sanctions of Sinai have lost their terrors' was surely a clear sign that mankind had reached the beginning of the end times when sin would be rampant, according to Jesus' prophecy in Matthew 24. When the commandments of God are dispensed with, a nation is doomed. But God in His love seeks to save souls. His commandments are not a list of prohibitions but signposts to peace and joy.

This is why at Kanaan we seek, in a variety of ways, to present the message of His commandments. Cast as a lifeline into the turbulent sea of the nations, it crosses linguistic and denominational barriers. As His Word is received in faith, souls are saved and added to the company of His faithful ones worldwide who, in the turmoil and deception of the end times, obey His commands and remain loyal to Jesus (Revelation 14:12).

The uncompromising proclamation of God's commandments as relevant for our times was not the only result of the Sinai experience. The Spirit of God, who calls into being that which does not exist, gave Mother Basilea at Mount Sinai a love for the nations of the world, such as she had never known before. So when, a few years later, requests came from one country after the other for a branch, she responded: sisters were sent abroad. But God is no one's debtor. Soon not only were Sisters of Mary serving abroad, but also, since 1968, more and more young girls from other countries have been called of God into our sisterhood.

At the time of writing 19 different nations are represented in our spiritual family. This, too, has been God's provision for carrying our ministry further afield. Some of our sisters from abroad are actively involved in producing foreign editions of our literature and videos. And all intercede for their native land, sharing in the joys and sorrows of their people.

As a family of sisters we are daily challenged to 'bear one another's burdens' (Galatians 6:2). In community life with its give and take, this verse becomes especially meaningful. In view of our different national and cultural backgrounds, misunderstandings are only natural. Yet we have found the sheer diversity of our fellowship an enrichment — a gift of our heavenly Father.

*Far left: Mother Basilea on Mount Sinai, 1963*

*Above: sisters serving abroad*

*Left: sisters from abroad*

# from Greenland ...

... to the African Bush

**Sri Lanka:** 'I am 20 years old, a student...I was an active member of the Transcendental Meditation movement. I joined ... to become free from stress and frustration. But when I was handling my day to day life with my family, relatives and friends, the stress and frustrations increased into a climax. In this situation one of my cousins gave me a leaflet, *A New Era*, written by M. Basilea Schlink. I read it carefully. Then only I came to realize about my actual situation. So I stopped going to meditation. I prayed to the Lord Jesus and offered every area of my life to be controlled by Him. Slowly I began to feel the true peace and happiness which only can be given by Jesus Christ. So now I am a completely changed person.'

❖

**Brazil:** 'You will be pleased to hear that as a result of reading your booklet *Rock Music — Where from, Where to?* many teenagers at our school have left their gangs and started a new life. Some of them have even started going to church — praise God!'

❖

**Holland:** 'I was with the Hare Krishnas, and one Sunday I went out on the streets with them. There I received a copy of the leaflet *And They Knew Not* and read it. Then the Lord helped me to come out of the movement and led me into a church, where I gave my life to the Lord Jesus. Since then I have been truly happy.'

❖

**Germany:** A young man with AIDS received one of our evangelistic leaflets in hospital. From then on he wanted to have the cover picture (the return of the prodigal) in a place where he could always see it. And the prayer inside became his own prayer, which he would pray fervently again and again. In the last stages of his illness he watched the Kanaan video *It Began at a Party*. When he saw again the picture of the father embracing the prodigal son, he said with tears, 'Lord, forgive me my sin and help me.' Shortly afterwards he died peacefully. The nurse placed the picture of the merciful father at the head of his bed.

❖

**Korea:** A doctor distributed about 10,000 copies of the leaflet *Don't End It All!* outside schools. Some weeks later she reported: 'Since then there have been no more suicides among the students in our town. They have warned each other of the dire consequences of such a step and of the reality of hell.'

❖

**Kenya:** 'The tracts you sent to me have been a blessing to many people...These tracts have brought revival in my area.'

❖

**Japan:** 'Up till now I couldn't care less whether there was a God or not. But your newspaper article "Joy Through Repentance and Reconciliation" really moved me, stirring me to the depths. The tears kept flowing. Repentance — what a profound word! I realized how arrogant I had been. Although I didn't have a clue how to pray, I felt impelled to ask forgiveness of God for the way I had been behaving...I want to know more about God. Please help me.'

❖

**Germany:** 'Many years ago my husband and I were challenged at Kanaan by the message of God's commandments, as if we had been hit by lightning. In our village we had two stationery shops. Our main income came from magazines and a lending library. But the contents became increasingly filthy. So we informed our

104

customers we would be discontinuing the sale and loan of such reading materials. Our announcement came like a bombshell! We should have run into debt and gone bankrupt. However, at the end of the year we were better off financially than when selling trash and smut. And this blessing has increased over the years.'

❖

**India:** At a Hindu festival Christians were handing out the tract *Jesus' Offer to You* in the Telugu language. On the second day of the festival the eldest son of a late priest at a big Hindu temple, who was under training to take his father's place, read the tract and gave it to his wife and four brothers. They read it, too, and afterwards all accepted Christ into their lives.

'Twenty-two young men who were sent by the authorities of the biggest Sri Rama Temple…as delegates to attend the big festival …read the tract. All of them felt that…the only true Saviour is Christ. They all accepted Christ as their only personal Saviour and the Lord. After conducting…regular Bible classes for them, we baptized them.'

❖

**Japan:** Our sisters there report: 'It is a special joy for us to see what God has done in the life of a young girl whom we met while hand-ing out leaflets against the musical *Jesus Christ Superstar*. At that time she received a copy of the leaflet *Where Can We Find Jesus?* She wrote us a very moving response afterwards and asked about the true God. At Christmas she was baptized along with her sister.

'A completely unreligious high-school teacher from northern Japan accidentally came across the book *My All for Him* in a Christian bookstore. Jesus drew so close to him in this book that he surrendered his whole life to Him. His wife, seeing the transformation in his life as he read more of our literature, also found Jesus.'

❖

**Norway:** 'The name of Jesus saved me when I was behind bars. Only this name has saving power,' a young man, who had been jailed for murder, testified at an Open Guest Day in our Norwe-gian branch. 'After my release my greatest wish was to get to know the place from where literature came to me while I was in prison.' Now he is actively involved in saving others as a soldier in the Salvation Army and hands out our literature to street kids.

❖

**Australia:** 'We have found your literature very helpful in the pris-ons. One young prisoner…was on the point of suicide when we sent him a Gospel of John together with…[several Kanaan leaflets are listed]. His response was tremendous in that he decided to utterly surrender to Jesus…and…to renounce all demonic and occult involvement…The girl he was living with at the time of his offence has become a Christian since his imprisonment and we recently attended their wedding in the prison.'

❖

**Brazil:** 'Recently I got into a conversation with my neighbour… Her marriage was at the point of breaking up. Suddenly I was reminded that in my Bible I had the leaflet *He Replies When I Call*… My neighbour took the leaflet with her and, as she read it, her heart grew softer and softer until tears of contrition ran down her cheeks. That evening she shared with her husband about what had happened. He wanted to read the leaflet as well — and had the same experience. Through the repentance of husband and wife their marriage was healed by the Lord.'

105

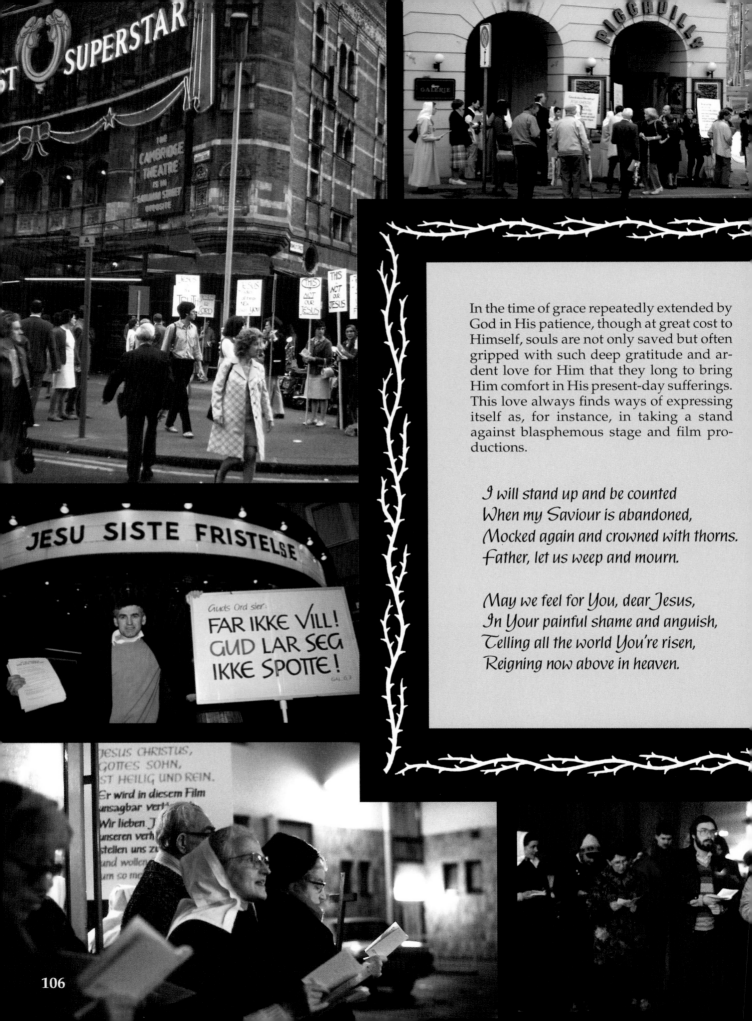

In the time of grace repeatedly extended by God in His patience, though at great cost to Himself, souls are not only saved but often gripped with such deep gratitude and ardent love for Him that they long to bring Him comfort in His present-day sufferings. This love always finds ways of expressing itself as, for instance, in taking a stand against blasphemous stage and film productions.

*I will stand up and be counted*
*When my Saviour is abandoned,*
*Mocked again and crowned with thorns.*
*Father, let us weep and mourn.*

*May we feel for You, dear Jesus,*
*In Your painful shame and anguish,*
*Telling all the world You're risen,*
*Reigning now above in heaven.*

劇団四季

ジーザス・クライスト
＝スーパースター

Jesus Christ Superstar

Church Declares 'Last Temptation' Morally Offensive

FILM: 25,000 Protest Against 'Last Temptation' at Universal

RELIGION

'...tack' on Christ

Universal Asked to 'Destroy' Scorsese's Film About Christ

A MOVIE'S CRIME

THE TEMP...

Luxury Theaters refuses to book 'Last Temptation'

Los Angeles Times CALENDAR

'The Last Temptation of Christ'

JESUS

Ministers won't bow to 'Temptation'

Religious movie is sacrilegious

BIG BUSINESS

PLEASE DO NOT WATCH SUCH BLASPHEMY

I PROTECT CHILDREN FROM BLASPHEMY

CHRIST IS THE SON OF GOD PURE AND HOLY

WE REPRESENT MILLIONS WHO LOVE & HONOUR JESUS CHRIST WE ARE DEEPLY GRIEVED OVER THIS FILM PLEASE DO NOT SEE IT

THE LAST TEMPTATION OF CHRIST

# A Race Against the Forces of Darkness

1980 — for years occult, pornographic and blasphemous stage and screen productions had been deluging the Western world. Millions were being presented with a distorted image of God. Sensing the deep pain in God's heart, Mother Basilea prayed for new ways of reaching as many as possible with the true image of God. If Satan can succeed in corrupting humanity so rapidly through stage and screen, could not God find people on fire to use the same media to call many back to His loving heart? The Lord answered, though differently and faster than we could have imagined.

It was mid-November. Mother Basilea was staying at our American branch, 'Canaan in the Desert', when a video distributor for television stations requested a programme with a profound Christmas message. In two weeks the video tape would have to be ready. Mother Basilea agreed, though at that time we were not even sure what 'video' was.

Against all probability, our first video programme *Jesus, Beloved Child* was televised that Christmas — not only in the United States but also in Canada, Australia, Kenya, and Italy — in English, Spanish and Italian. The Child Jesus had set the video ministry in motion. We were further challenged by a Canaan Friend in America, 'How will you sisters give account

1 Video distributor

2 American Canaan Friend

3 Filming of our first Christmas programme

4 Filming during Mother Basilea's talk at Providence, Rhode Island (USA), 1982

5 Visiting a television station

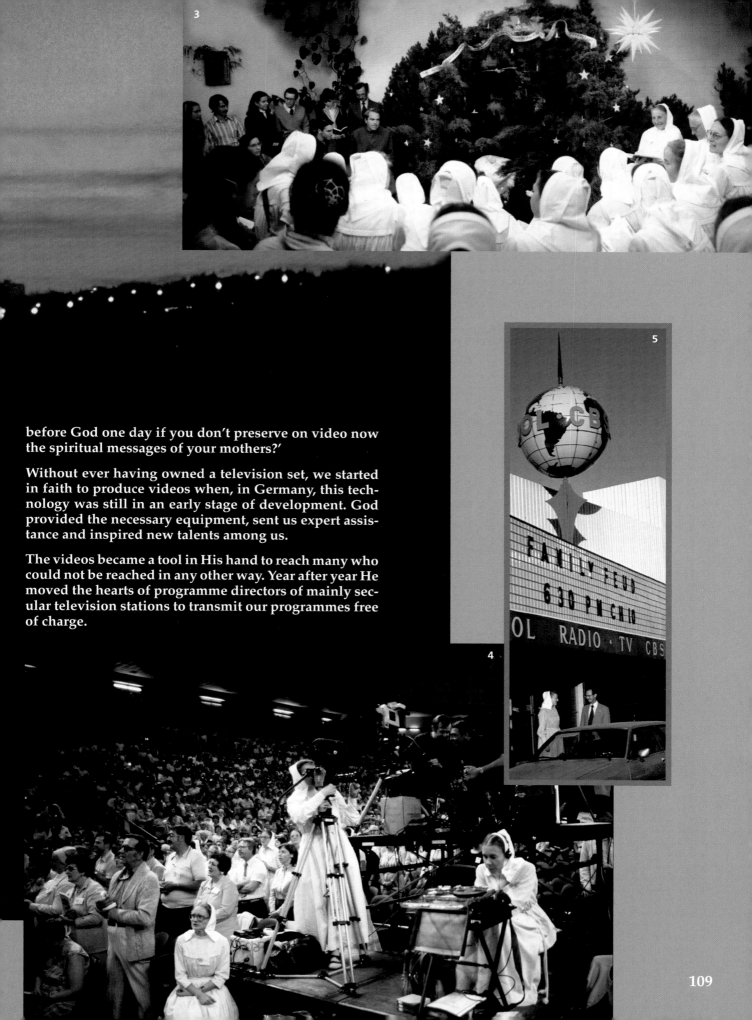

before God one day if you don't preserve on video now the spiritual messages of your mothers?'

Without ever having owned a television set, we started in faith to produce videos when, in Germany, this technology was still in an early stage of development. God provided the necessary equipment, sent us expert assistance and inspired new talents among us.

The videos became a tool in His hand to reach many who could not be reached in any other way. Year after year He moved the hearts of programme directors of mainly secular television stations to transmit our programmes free of charge.

## Today we have video programmes in 23 languages transmitted on all five contine

'This film is a guide for young people who have never known a mother's love.'   Costa Rica

'I was lost, heading for hell with no hope of salvation and couldn't care less. I was into drugs, alcohol … I sat there on my sofa watching …Then the Lord Jesus touched my heart …Your words reached me … and through you God saved my life from hell. Jesus changed my whole life from that moment on. My bitter heart just melted away…As soon as I gave my life to Christ, my marriage was healed instantly (it was on the rocks near destruction) …'   USA

'Your messages are as simple as water and as bold as lightning; and they show us that God has not completely withdrawn from this pagan and secularized world of ours.'   Honduras

'We…really enjoyed all the telecasts prepared by your ministry. It was really heart-touching and we are hoping that you would telecast more of this sort of programmes so that all the people on this earth would repent and accept Jesus as their only personal Lord and Saviour, including myself and my family.'   Fiji Islands

'You can't imagine how comforting your words are as I begin my day. Your daily message gives me hope and brings me close to God.'   Puerto Rico

'Her words about Jesus' love brought me peace and hope. I wish to know Him more, love Him more, and serve Him more.'   Philippines

'I've been waiting for a show like that … I'm 15 years old.'   USA

Minister: 'I was looking for something to be wrong — to be suspicious of, but found nothing … Love for Jesus shines through everywhere.'   Canada

'I sense it was a call of Jesus Christ — and a new light has come into my life.'   Brazil

'A truly beautiful programme … It answered many questions for me. I am a mother of three sons and many times they ask questions and I might not have an answer for them, but I did receive an answer — go back to the basics! Our answer lies in the Ten Commandments.'   USA

Bus-driver: 'Because the hope given in your programme is missing in the television news, you sit there afterwards, overwhelmed by all the suffering and misery in the

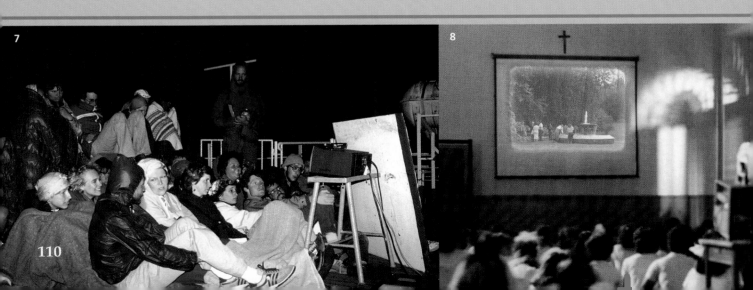

## hundreds of stations ... From an abundance of responses here is a selection:

world. I've got to see all the other Kanaan videos as soon as possible — best of all this very day. Why didn't anyone tell me about this message before?'     Norway

'I had strayed far away from God. Through the film I was challenged to sort out my life and go in the right direction again.'
Costa Rica

'I wanted to run away, because the situation in our family was so awful. But then I saw your film and experienced that God is alive and can change everything! I found the courage to face life again. Now everything is different.'
Singapore

Prison inmate: 'Everything that was said touched my heart in faith…It really made my Christmas the best in many years.' USA

'I wish I knew how to express gratitude enough for the programme …*When God's Heart Breaks with Love*. There is so much that bears the name "Christian" but has deceptive content, or none at all…This was material that could lift an individual, a TV station, or nation to a quiet and victorious confidence in God … Please make way for more.'
Australia

Minister: 'Your message is what the world so desperately needs.'
USA

'So rarely have I witnessed such joy in God's loving presence during a liturgy.'     Canada

'Watched your television show of reconciliation messages on TV recently. We are Buddhists and we greatly enjoyed your "preaching" and showing of love and forgiveness.'     Australia

A 17-year-old: 'I want you to know that I'm a different Priscilla now. I have begun a new life with God — and with my family.'     Costa Rica

1,4 Kanaan co-workers preparing for
    filming and in the video studio
2   Working with 16mm film
3   Video recording for television spots
5   Filming at Kanaan
6   Subtitling Swedish programmes
7   Aboard ship in the Mediterranean
8   In a Brazilian school
9   Togo: film show in a village; the chief,
    his family and 170 villagers find Jesus

# I, I AM HE THAT COMFORTS YOU. Isaiah 51:12

# FATHER OF COMFORT

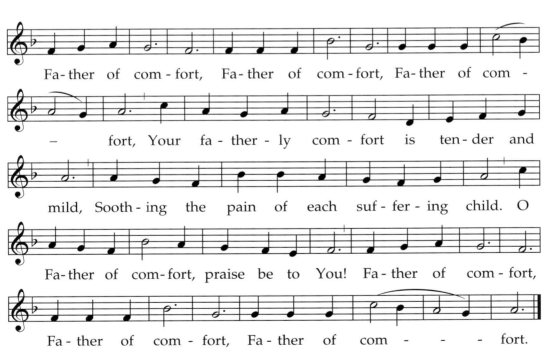

Fa-ther of com-fort, Fa-ther of com-fort, Fa-ther of com- - fort, Your fa-ther-ly com-fort is ten-der and mild, Sooth-ing the pain of each suf-fer-ing child. O Fa-ther of com-fort, praise be to You! Fa-ther of com-fort, Fa-ther of com-fort, Fa-ther of com - - - fort.

**B**lessed be the God and Father of our Lord Jesus Christ, the Father of mercies and God of all comfort, who comforts us in all our affliction, so that we may be able to comfort those who are in any affliction, with the comfort with which we ourselves are comforted by God.

2 Corinthians 1:3-4

In 1979 a new chapter began in our community. Never had we so needed the comfort of the Father and never did we experience it so abundantly as at this time. Over the years requests had come from various parts of the world for additional branches to be opened. Owing to the growth of our ministry at Kanaan, it had not been possible to accept these invitations. But now the Lord showed that the time was right.

As always, when faced with a commission from God, our mothers looked beyond the impossibilities. However, they clearly realized that it was an either-or situation. Either they could send a large number of sisters abroad to start new branches; or else they could keep everything going at home the way it was.

The decision was made to curtail many of our activities. Retreats, Herald Plays, and various celebrations were discontinued. The printing and distribution of our German books was entrusted to a Christian publishing house in Stuttgart (Christliches Verlagshaus). Some of the buildings at Kanaan were rented out for a lengthy period to Evangelical Christian/Baptist families of German origin returning from the then Soviet Union; for ten years they had the use of the Herald Chapel for their meetings.

At that time many of us were asked if we were prepared to follow the Lord's call to another country, even though it meant leaving our spiritual home here. Over a period of months one commissioning service after the other was held: an unforgettable time that left behind a deep gap in our spiritual family, linked as we are by warm bonds of fellowship in Jesus.

The sisters, mainly young, were uprooted from the security of the Mother House and planted in foreign countries and cultures — sometimes only in twos, often with little or no knowledge of the language, without a large circle of friends, and helpless in many respects. In this situation an anthem sung during the ceremony when we receive our habits became especially meaningful:

> Wherever you go, I will go;
> wherever you live, I will live.
> Your people will be my people.
>
> Ruth 1:16 GNB

But the God of all comfort also drew near to the 'little flock' left at Kanaan, because cutting back is, in some aspects, harder than developing a ministry. According to human standards our way of life has never been secure, yet now the future seemed more uncertain than ever. In addition, our mothers were often abroad to support our

Seid dankbar in allen Dingen

As our numbers and ministries grew again, the Lord gave us back our houses and the Herald Chapel. The repatriates built their own church-cum-community centre ... Although in various ways Kanaan in 1997 is different, the nature of its ministries having changed, once more numerous visitors join us for our worship services, prayer services and celebrations.

*With Your hands so kind and holy,*
*O my Father, You will guide me*
*On each pathway to its goal.*
*And Your child is filled with wonder,*
*For Your plans and deeds and counsels*
*Are a masterpiece of love.*

sisters in their new start. That we could still be joyful is thanks to the Father of comfort. Whoever clings to His hand will not falter, even in the dark.

Soon we were abundantly comforted, both inwardly and outwardly. After this difficult transitional period, a large number of young sisters joined, mainly from abroad, so that lack of space became acute again. And what a surprise it was when we found ourselves producing our first television programme, which developed into an extensive film and video ministry! While we still tended to look with regret on former years, when visitors came in droves, the Lord already had in mind the countless numbers worldwide we would never have reached in any other way. Unimagined opportunities also opened up for our literature ministry as a result of the political changes that swept through Eastern Europe.

---

1   *Repatriated Evangelical Christians / Baptists at Kanaan*

2-3  *Herald Chapel used as their meeting place*

4   *Bas-relief, Mother House entrance.*
    *Text: 'And he arose and came to his father ...'*

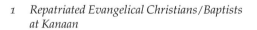

# COMFORT, COMFORT MY PEOPLE...

*Isaiah 40:*

In Talpiot, Jerusalem, we have a house, Beth Abraham, where we have been privileged to minister comfort for over 35 years. Whom would we rather comfort than those against whom we have sinned immeasurably as a nation? How thankful we are to God for so abundantly blessing this ministry, even though it can never be more than a drop in the ocean.

Over the years Holocaust survivors have been strengthened in Beth Abraham. Deep wounds of the soul have begun to heal. Our sisters are always put to shame by the forgiving love and humble gratitude of their guests. 'In Beth Abraham we are privileged to welcome saints and martyrs. They are such a blessing to us.'

A response such as the following never fails to move us deeply:

'This week offered us many opportunities to discover miracles of God abou which we had known nothing. Who could have imagined this during th afflictions of the Nazi era? The Nazis were determined to wipe out anything associated with the word "Jew". Who could have guessed that people c integrity, true friends and lovers of Israel would emerge from among th Germans?...

'We also received much love from foreign visitors whom we met during ou stay here. You have no idea what you mean to the Jewish people because c

your work! Your faith has won our hearts. You and we believe in one God. Now when it is time to say good-bye, we all feel as if we were parting from close family members.

'We are praying that the scripture will be fulfilled: "And he will come to Zion as Redeemer" (Isaiah 59:20). All of us are to experience the Messiah coming with haste in our times. Amen.'

1 *Beth Abraham, Talpiot, Jerusalem*
2 *Relaxing in the garden*
3 *Last-minute farewell*
4 *Visiting the kitchen*
5 *Celebrating with guests*
6 *Feast of Tabernacles*
7 *Closing session*

# My Father, I do not understand You, but I trust in Your love.

So prayed Mother Basilea in the darkest hour of her life. The power of this prayer corresponds to the depths out of which it was born. How often God has used these few words to minister to those in despair when nothing else could reach their hearts.

Today plaques and leaflets, all with words of comfort, can be found at many cemeteries. What a unique opportunity, for cemeteries daily bear witness to much heartache and grief.

One testimony reads: 'My beloved husband had died. In deep sorrow I went for a walk on Saturday and happened to pass by a cemetery. A box containing tracts was attached to a tree. I took out the leaflet *Strengthened All Week Long*. The reading for Saturday was: "God has taken away the person dearest to you — someone who meant everything to you, the joy of your life. You say you cannot live without this person. Hear the Lord saying in your heart, 'I have taken from you someone who is precious to you, so as to give you Someone infinitely greater and dearer: Myself…'" I read the words over and over again, until I understood and had faith. Jesus has become my one and all. My life belongs entirely to Him! Today — two years later — I wanted to write and share this with you, so as to encourage you to go on distributing …'

In recent years the ministry of bringing comfort has spread. Both local and national newspapers have been printing, free of charge, short comforting texts next to the death announcements and obituaries. In a Christian news magazine, an article entitled 'Comfort from the Press' cited the managing director of a large German daily as saying: 'Particularly in the area of bereavement and death we consider it important for our readers to be encouraged to reflect on life positively.' The article went on to quote readers' responses: 'I would like to express my gratitude that in our newspaper … there are texts bringing light and comfort in the dark valley of sorrow and mourning.' — 'The normal business-like style of a newspaper consequently acquires a pleasant, humane, sympathetic face.'

These short texts are translated into approximately 90 languages and distributed worldwide.

JESUS CHRISTUS SPRICHT:

ICH BIN DIE
AUFERSTEHUNG
UND DAS LEBEN.
WER AN MICH
GLAUBET,
DER WIRD LEBEN,
OB ER GLEICH—
STÜRBE. Johannes 11,25

Bei Gott ist das Leid
nie das Letzte.

Ein Wort für Dich—
greif zu!

IM **JA**
ZUM WILLEN
GOTTES
VERLIERT
DAS LEIDEN
SEINE
MACHT. MB

Ein Wort für Dich—
greif zu!

I AM
THE RESURRECTION
AND THE LIFE;
HE WHO BELIEVES IN ME,
THOUGH HE DIE,
YET SHALL HE LIVE.
JOHN 11:25

With God suffering is never
the final outcome. MB

People are suffering the world over, with growing numbers coming under the cross of persecution and often in peril of their lives. Will not the heavenly Father single out such souls for His comfort?

Again, it was a story of small beginnings. In an attic room of the Mother House the first small offset machine was operated. In the cellar of the house 'Jesus' Comfort' — despite constant interruptions from background noise! — we attempted the first 'studio recordings'.

As early as 1952 the Lord had shown that He wanted to call a 'worldwide ministry' into being. In faith we made a sign with these words, and there it hung on our first letterpress, often to the embarrassment of our sisters in the print-shop when visitors

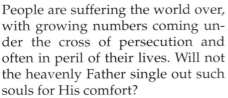

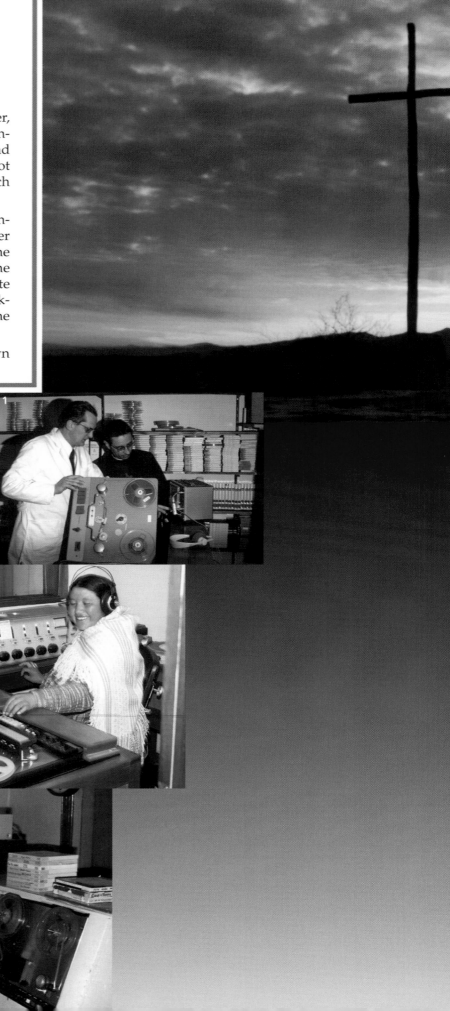

came. We had virtually no translations, no prospect of foreign guests — even a bus-load of people from our state of Hesse was unusual. But to the comforting love of God there are no boundaries or obstacles.

At present books and pamphlets from Kanaan are available in over 60 languages, and there are approximately 300 radio transmissions weekly in 12 languages... The Kanaan message penetrated the Iron and Bamboo Curtains, reaching even areas considered inaccessible. Soon our print-shop and publishing department could no longer meet all the demands. We needed believers on the spot who could care for the spreading of the message in their own countries. To this day our materials are translated, printed, produced, transmitted and restocked — even under persecution and sometimes for years on end unbeknown to us.

Since the Iron Curtain has opened and relief convoys have been travelling to the former Eastern-bloc countries requests for Kanaan literature in the different languages have increased. Books, leaflets and short texts by the million have now found their way into Russia (even faraway Siberia and beyond the Arctic Circle) and other CIS states, the Baltic states, Mongolia, Albania, Romania, Bulgaria … A completely new branch in our ministry has sprung up. And yet it is all insufficient. This is why we keep praying for more helping hands and that Jesus will bless all the efforts a hundredfold, so that the miracle of the 'multiplication of the loaves' will be constantly repeated and that there will be spiritual food enough — and to spare.

1  Recording studio, Kanaan
2  Bolivia
3  El Salvador
4  Beginnings of the printing ministry,
   Mother House attic
5  First letterpress, Kanaan print-shop
6  Estonia
7  Ghana

Weltweite Sendung+

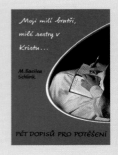

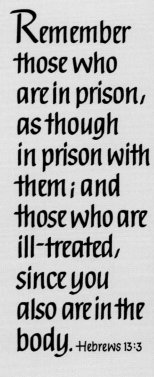

Remember those who are in prison, as though in prison with them; and those who are ill-treated, since you also are in the body. Hebrews 13:3

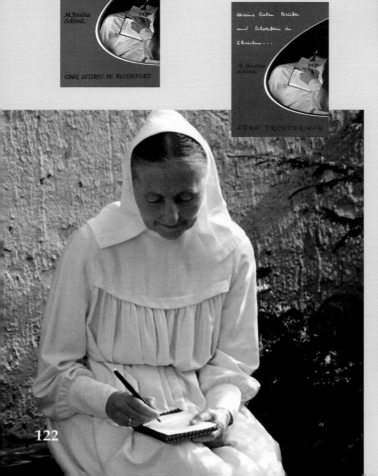

# Dear Brothers and Sisters in Christ...

This is the title of a small collection of comforting letters Mother Basilea wrote in ardent love and sympathy for our persecuted fellow-Christians. So far none of these letters has been applicable to us here in the West, our ultimate time of testing not yet having come. We can still witness openly. But, according to Holy Scripture, all who want to follow Jesus are bound to suffer persecution (2 Timothy 3:12). Surely those who already have the honour of suffering for His name's sake deserve our special prayer support.

The five letters of comfort have been distributed in many languages since 1978. Yet few of those for whom they were written were able to respond. Probably only in eternity will we hear the full story of those who have come out of great affliction.

Whoever went to have a talk with Mother Martyria in her room could not help but notice a poster displaying photos of imprisoned Christians, with their name, age, and length of prison sentence. Constantly updated, this poster was an essential part of Mother Martyria's prayer life. And this is how even the youngest sister came to be gripped with love for the suffering Body of Christ on earth and learnt to intercede specifically for individual Christians under persecution. At the same time Mother Martyria would teach us to pray for ourselves in view of the future:

Lord Jesus,
help me to live
in such a way today
that I can endure
suffering for You
tomorrow.

123

124

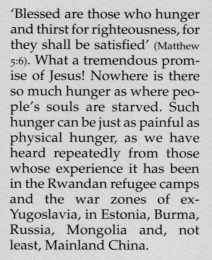

'Blessed are those who hunger and thirst for righteousness, for they shall be satisfied' (Matthew 5:6). What a tremendous promise of Jesus! Nowhere is there so much hunger as where people's souls are starved. Such hunger can be just as painful as physical hunger, as we have heard repeatedly from those whose experience it has been in the Rwandan refugee camps and the war zones of ex-Yugoslavia, in Estonia, Burma, Russia, Mongolia and, not least, Mainland China.

But the famous Great Wall of China has, figuratively speaking, been leapt over many times. For the love of God, even the highest walls are no hindrance.

'How God must love the Chinese, otherwise He wouldn't have created so many millions of them' — the disarming logic of a Chinese friend. We seek to do all we can for these souls, in whose midst Jesus is glorified, demonstrating His power in deepest affliction. Many times couriers have taken the five letters of comfort and other literature across the border. They have brought into the country audio and video cassettes, which are being duplicated there. At night-time outreaches the short texts are passed from hand to hand. And for over 25 years 'Call from Kanaan' has been reaching China's vast territories through radio. It is hard to imagine what this spiritual food means for the people there: 'Thank you for giving us the opportunity to know God. Sometimes we are so carried away that we forget to eat and sleep.' — 'I am glad that we can meet over the air.'

1-2 'Come over ... and help us' (Acts 16:9)

3-5 Christians in China, Burma and Mongolia

*N*o eye has seen, nor ear heard,
nor the heart of man conceived,
what *G*od has prepared for those who love hi

1 Corinthians 2:9

Because the joy of heaven begins here and now, we celebrate festivals of heaven at Kanaan, representing as vividly as possible what it will be like. The overcomers at the throne are described as holding palm branches (Revelation 7:9) and so, young and old alike, we pass through 'the pearly gates', branches in hand, full of eager expectation.

The darker it becomes on earth, the more we want to celebrate and to affirm our heavenly citizenship (Philippians 3:20), worshipping and thanking God for what His love has prepared for us. One of Mother Basilea's dearest wishes is that the joyful expectation of heaven will never cease among us and that many

others will be drawn into the hope of the heavenly glory. Such an attitude always helps to put the sufferings of this age in proper perspective (Romans 8:18).

✣

*Sing of heaven*
*when you are least in the*
*mood for singing.*
*Sing of heaven,*
*and heaven will come down.*

# GREAT IS YOUR FAITHFULNESS.

Lamentations 3:23 RAV

FATHER OF FAITHFULNESS

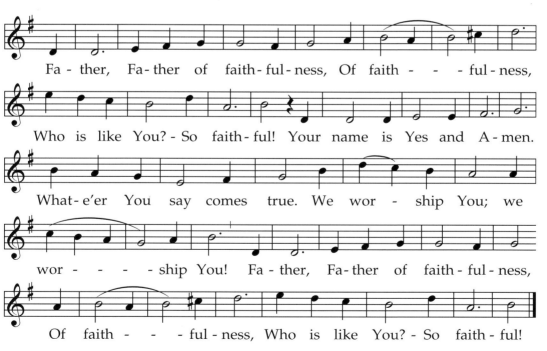

Fa - ther, Fa - ther of faith - ful - ness, Of faith - - - ful - ness,

Who is like You? - So faith - ful! Your name is Yes and A - men.

What - e'er You say comes true. We wor - ship You; we

wor - - - - ship You! Fa - ther, Fa - ther of faith - ful - ness,

Of faith - - - ful - ness, Who is like You? - So faith - ful!

## God Is Faithful

The longer we follow the Lord, the more deeply we appreciate that God is a Father of faithfulness. Those of us who have served the Lord in our sisterhood for 30 or 40, even 50, years now can especially testify to that.

Human loyalty is often quick to come to an end, threatened by each disappointment, as is tragically evident in this age of increasing unfaithfulness. We only have to look at ourselves to know how deceitful and lacking in integrity is the human heart (Jeremiah 17:9).

But *one* heart is different, totally different. 'God is faithful' (1 Corinthians 1:9). How often Mother Martyria has challenged us to respond to God's faithfulness by being faithful ourselves. To a ripe old age she has consistently lived out and testified, 'Be true to the Lord at all costs, for it's where we stand in the end that counts.'

Fa - ther, You have always helped me, lov-ing Fa - ther that You are,

All these years Your hand up - on me right up to this ve - ry hour,

Ever faithful, ever loving, gently guiding day and night,
For the smallest details caring, as a father would provide.

Just as the water continually flows over from the upper bowl of the Fountain of the Father's Goodness, so does the Father's heart overflow with love for His children. In four of our overseas branches such a fountain can be found proclaiming the unchanging faithfulness of God. In His loving fatherly care He brightens

...he often difficult everyday life of our sisters
in the branches, far away from the security of
the Mother House with the many helping
hands of our large family.

*Top left: Paraguay / Top right: Taiwan*
*Bottom left: Australia / Bottom right: USA*

Painful though the Father's chastening and His acts of judgment are,
They are tokens of His blessing as He draws me to His heart;
From the snares of this world freeing like a good and trusty friend,
In His holy, saving love through the cross me homewards leading.
All things here are transient. Love divine will never end. Paul Gerhardt (1607-1676)

Reflecting on the 50 years since the Sisterhood of Mary began, we never cease to be amazed at God's faithfulness in view of our apathy, resistance and lack of love. Over the years He has repeatedly reached out to us in love until our hardened hearts softened and we could hear what He was saying to us. The heavenly Father sometimes uses external events to help us recognize the state of our hearts and to turn to Him in repentance. One stormy night, for instance, the tallest poplar at Kanaan was blown down. Since then a plaque in the Mother House prayer garden reminds us that God will humble all who are proud and conceited (Isaiah 2:12).

Prior to our twenty-fifth anniversary, which was to be marked by a festival celebrating the love of Jesus, Mother Basilea likened our spiritual preparation to doing the washing or spring-cleaning. During such a cleansing God will even act against His own interests — or so it seems. For the sake of our souls He will sometimes go so far as to allow a shadow to fall upon His glory.

How could it be any different before our fiftieth anniversary? This time, too, God has had to put us through a refining process and shake us out of our complacency. He allowed one of our branches to suffer from flooding in the workrooms, and another from a fire in its nearby book depot. Though His wrath endures but for a moment and His grace lasts for ever, as we have discovered in all His dealings, there is an ache in our hearts that we burden Him with our sins.

Included is the pain that, in the course of these 50 years, some who had been with us for a long time have turned back, giving up their calling. Jesus knows our human weakness — now as then. Long ago He asked His disciples, 'Will you also go away?' (John 6:67). Probably no ministry in the Kingdom of God is spared such experiences. Yet always greater than every failure, every painful disappointment in oneself and in one another, is the truth:

'Through the Lord's mercies we are not consumed, because his compassions fail not. They are new every morning; great is your faithfulness.'
Lamentations 3:22-23

The rainbow represents God's constant, unfailing love.
Against the backdrop of our sin it shines most radiantly, for God is both
Author and Finisher.
If a human artist can hardly bear to leave a work unfinished,
how much more will the eternal God complete the work He has begun
in those who belong to Him (Philippians 1:6)!

*Rainbow over 'Canaan in the Desert', Phoenix, Arizona (USA)*

Holy and sublime, the Father reigns in majesty and power o'er confusion and distress.
When we seem to walk in darkness, God the Father reassures us that His plans are wonderful.
Let us praise and worship humbly God's eternal plan so loving, which determines all our paths.
Those who trust Him without wav'ring soon will understand His leadings. He fulfils them gloriously.

*Taken from: 'My Father, I Trust You'*

GIVING GOD
GLORY is man's
highest calling.
God alone is worthy
of glory, for He is
the almighty, all-
knowing, all-loving
Lord who made us.
Rejoice in this calling.
Give God glory
and He will draw
close to you.

Photo: dpa

On Obersalzberg, near Berchtesgaden, Bavaria, where Hitler had his mountain retreat, God was not glorified. Here lived a man who wanted to be like God — a man who brought death and destruction to vast numbers with the Third Reich. In 1964, on Rossfeld, not far from this site of human madness and arrogance, we were able to erect the Noah Monument glorifying God in His faithfulness.

In the days of Noah, God ended the doings of the wicked through the Great Flood. Yet He did not destroy the earth entirely. He delivered Noah and his family, making a covenant with them, which holds good to this day (Genesis 8:21-22). Through Noah, who led a life of godly fear and obedience as a man after God's own heart, humanity was spared total destruction. God longs to temper judgment with mercy: He extends the time of grace when He finds even a few God-fearing souls (Genesis 18:25-32).

In the New Testament the challenge rings out: 'Fear God and give him glory, for the hour of his judgment has come; and worship him who made heaven and earth…' (Revelation 14:7*). An 'eternal gospel' to be proclaimed to all nations, tribes, tongues and peoples, this scripture was of particular significance for Mother Basilea, becoming the basis of our praise ministry.

We will probably never know how much our praise and thanksgiving means to the heart of God today when the hour of His judgment has begun. Because nothing is harder for the love of God than executing judgment, may our singing, worship and thanksgiving be a consolation to Him in His pain. In our times, when humanity is on a self-destructive course, having largely turned its back on God, let us pray:

*O Father, extend the time of grace for Your world and let not the beauty of Your creation be ruined. Rather than spoil the work of Your hands through sin, we want to praise and glorify You.**

Noah Monument, Rossfeld, near Berchtesgaden. Inscription in text above*

1 Nufenen Pass, Switzerland

2 Warragamba Dam, Australia

3 Birnau, Lake Constance, Germany

4 Lorelei on the Rhine, Germany

5 Malawi

6 Korea

7 Mandai Orchid Gardens, Singapore

8 Swedish plaque, Finnish

9 Indian Ocean, South Afri coast

10 Iguaçu Falls, Brazil

11 Taiwan

12 Near Zermatt, Switzerlar

13 Japan

14 Finland

15 Lake Riesach, Austria

10

11

15

12

13

14

'How charming!' was the comment of the director of our first film, upon seeing some praise plaques. 'Who came up with this delightful idea?' But it was not just some delightful idea. Rather was it an inspiration of the Holy Spirit. And what is of God always prevails in the end. In this day and age, when countless numbers blaspheme God, declare Him to be dead and try to eliminate everything reminiscent of Him, the Lord brought the praise ministry into being. Like a divine seal, praise plaques now mark many of the world's best-known scenic spots. Challenged by their message, people have turned back to the One who made the earth so beautiful and who sustains it to this day.

# Die Ostschweiz

**REGIONALAUSGABE FÜRSTENLAND/UNTERTOGGENBURG**

## PTT-Gewinn soll auf 200 Mio steigen

BERN. Der «Gelbe Riese» rechnet für 1994 mit einem Gewinn von fast 200 Millionen Franken. Der Verwaltungsrat der PTT verabschiedete gestern das Budget für 1994, das von einem Wachstum der Nachfrage um 2,4 Prozent und einer weiteren Reduktion des Personalbestandes ausgeht. Für Beteiligungen an anderen Unternehmen stehen fast 360 Millionen Franken bereit.

☐ Der Entwurf des PTT-Finanzvoranschlags 1994 sieht einen Gesamtumsatzrekord von 14.622 Millionen Franken und Gesamtausgaben von 4,221 Mio Franken vor, vor der Presse machte die PTT-Leitung

*(remaining article text illegible)*

### Zu Ehren des ersten Bundespartners

Dedicated as places of never-ending praise, our praise chapels at Aeschi and Griesalp in Switzerland's Bernese Oberland are pillars of the praise ministry. For over 30 years sisters and friends have ministered there in the summer months. Hikers and tourists pause in the chapels for some quiet moments and the praise services draw many worshippers.

> We pray, Lord,
> let many hearts be fanned into flame;
> call multitudes, Lord, to praise Your great name,
> dedicating their lives to glorifying You.

If only praise plaques could speak! Occasionally, however, remarkable stories do reach us, indicating how God has used them. Take, for instance, a plaque on the south coast of England:

'I have suffered from bouts of depression for a number of years and ... I went to Beachy Head, fully intending to throw myself over the cliff. I was very drunk — I have had a drink problem for many years

oo. As I was staggering along the top of the cliffs, totally out of my head — I literally fell over a plaque, which I hadn't noticed. I won't tell you what I thought of whoever had put it in such a stupid place! Anyhow, I got up and decided to see what it was about and it read as follows:

> Mightier than the thunders of many waters,
> Mightier than the waves of the sea,
> The Lord on high is mighty! Psalm 93:4

> God is always greater than all of our troubles.

It was as if something snapped inside me and I sat and cried like a baby — anyone seeing me must have thought I was totally insane! I suddenly thought of my children and knew I couldn't do that to them, however desperate I was, so I rang my minister from the top of Beachy Head...'

Background: Praise chapel at Aeschi, Bernese Oberland, Switzerland — Switzerland's National Day: front-page article honouring God as the principal partner in the Swiss Confederation

1-3 Praise chapel at Griesalp-Steinenberg, Bernese Oberland, Switzerland

4 Near Beachy Head, England's south coast
5 Overlooking Aletsch Glacier, Switzerland
6 Time of praise at the Grand Canyon, USA
7 Oberammergau
8 Affixing praise plaque at Parpaner Rothorn, Grisons, Switzerland
9 On the way to Gorner Grat, Valais, Switzerland

143

Fill all the world
with song

Moosfluh, Aletsch region, Switzerland
Stained glass windows, praise chapel, Aeschi,
Switzerland

144

praise

## In Closing, We Can Only Say Thank You

We thank our heavenly Father for raising up our mothers to be His instruments. We thank Him for their yieldedness and for lovingly following Him in obedience inspired by faith:

**Mother Martyria** who with sacrificial love was always available for us sisters and brothers, day in, day out, supporting us in our everyday troubles and struggles and who through her words and faithful example helped us grow in our calling

**Mother Basilea** who, for love of God and in response to His call, would often withdraw from her many activities for lengthy times of prayer and solitude, thereby receiving an abundance of writings and songs that were to bless us and many others.

In gratitude for the spiritual riches the Lord has given us through our mothers, we would like to close with a final word from them personally, without which this book would not be complete.

The insights shared with us by our spiritual mothers reflect their distinctive personalities. But, in each case, what they said ministered to our hearts, they themselves being attuned to the heart of God. What follows is just a small part of the legacy of their lives. Our Lord Himself will ensure that the stream of blessing continues to flow ...

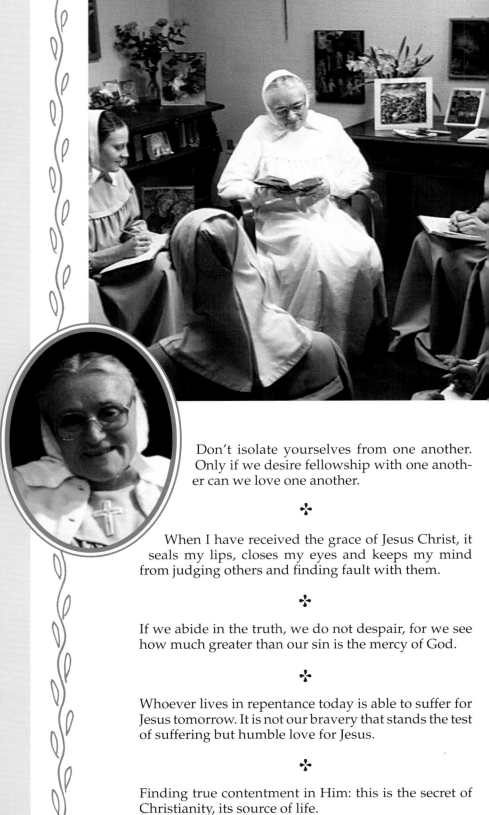

Don't isolate yourselves from one another. Only if we desire fellowship with one another can we love one another.

❖

When I have received the grace of Jesus Christ, it seals my lips, closes my eyes and keeps my mind from judging others and finding fault with them.

❖

If we abide in the truth, we do not despair, for we see how much greater than our sin is the mercy of God.

❖

Whoever lives in repentance today is able to suffer for Jesus tomorrow. It is not our bravery that stands the test of suffering but humble love for Jesus.

❖

Finding true contentment in Him: this is the secret of Christianity, its source of life.

❖

Only by bearing the cross do we enter the true fellowship of Jesus' love. Only on the pathway of the cross do we find deepest bliss and a foretaste of heaven.

My dear daughters and sons,

Do you know what the words 'trusting in His love' entail?

Do you know that the greatest gift a person can give God is trust in His love when all is dark?

Do you know that this is the greatest comfort for the Father's heart in view of the millions who in times of testing clench their fists, refusing to believe that His heart is love?

Believing in the love of God, when everything is against our doing so, needs to be learnt and practised. But this is only possible along dark pathways. There we will grow ever stronger so that even in the severest trials we have the strength to believe in His love …

Can you imagine the overwhelming awe in a person's heart when he finds that God really is Yes and Amen? This will be our experience in heaven when we see these words written over our lives. God's ultimate purpose behind many leadings will remain hidden to us on earth. Only in eternity will we realize that He was fulfilling His promises, pronouncing His Yes and Amen upon them and bringing everything to a glorious conclusion. God may be saving up His biggest surprises for heaven as a present for us, when He will reveal His deepest thoughts and plans …

Thanks be to our
**FATHER** in heaven,
whose
**MERCY**
delivered us out of the
ruins of our city and
planted us in a small
piece of land: Kanaan,
and whose fatherly
**GOODNESS**
has sustained us
and provided for us
to this day.
Thanks be to our Father,
who has loved us with
an infinite
**LOVE**
and who in His
**GRACE**
did not deal with us
as we deserved
because of our sins,
but in great
**PATIENCE**
never tired of rearing
and training His
children, and who has
continually encouraged
us with His
**COMFORT**
and whose
**FAITHFULNESS**
will surround us to
the end, ensuring that
His purposes are
fulfilled to His glory.

The LAMB
in the midst of the
throne will be their
shepherd, and he
will guide them
to springs of
living water;
and God will wipe away
every tear from
their eyes...
And he who sat upon
the throne said,
'Behold, I make
all things new.'

Revelation 7:17; 21:5

# CONTENTS

*(themes listed below do not necessarily appear as titles in the text)*

*Unless otherwise stated, prayers, songs and calligraphic texts are by M. Basilea Schlink.*

Literature by M. Basilea Schlink and M. Martyria Madauss* supplementary to the theme of this jubilee book:

## Father of Mercy

REPENTANCE: THE JOY-FILLED LIFE
An ongoing repentance is the basis for true joy.
96 pages

REALITIES: THE MIRACLES OF GOD EXPERIENCED TODAY
(American edition: *Realities of Faith*)
Testimonies of remarkable answers to prayer in near-impossible situations.
128 pages

## Father of Goodness

PRAYING OUR WAY THROUGH LIFE
48 pages

LET ME STAND AT YOUR SIDE
Accompanying Jesus in spirit from Gethsemane to Calvary.
160 pages

## Father of Love

STRONG IN THE TIME OF TESTING
*(quoted on p.61)*
In Jesus Christ we can find all the grace we need to stand the test of suffering.
96 pages

THE HOLY LAND TODAY
A guide to the places where Jesus lived and suffered.
368 pages, 5 sketch-maps

## Father of Grace

JESUS — A PORTRAIT OF LOVE*
A meditation on Matthias Grünewald's Isenheim Altar.
64 pages, hard cover, 28 colour plates

TURNING DEFEAT INTO VICTORY*
Discipleship in the light of Romans.
128 pages

THE CHRISTIAN'S VICTORY
(American edition:
*You Will Never Be the Same*)
Knowing the power of redemption in daily life.
192 pages

THE SECRET OF LOVING —
WHEN YOU CAN'T
24 pages

SONGS FOR SPIRITUAL WARFARE
48 pages

BUILDING A WALL OF PRAYER
An intercessor's handbook.
96 pages

MY ALL FOR HIM
*(quoted on p.76)*
Love for Jesus is the Christian's most prized treasure.
160 pages

BRIDE OF JESUS CHRIST
*(quoted on p.79)*
The ultimate which the love of God has planned for us.
64 pages

O NONE CAN BE LOVED LIKE JESUS
*(quoted on p.79)*
Songs of love for Jesus.
48 pages

MARY, THE MOTHER OF JESUS
The life of Mary as we know it from the Bible. A challenge to a closer walk with Jesus.
128 pages

ISRAEL, MY CHOSEN PEOPLE
A German confession before God and the Jews. The heartcry of one who realizes that to hurt the apple of God's eye is to hurt God Himself.
144 pages

## Father of Patience

GOD LAMENTS —
AND OUR RESPONSE
The calling of the end-time believers.
64 pages

I WANT TO CONSOLE YOU
Songs of love and comfort for our Lord in His suffering today.
72 pages

THE JOY OF MY HEART
Watchwords interpreting God's commandments in everyday life.
38 pages

MORE PRECIOUS THAN GOLD
Daily readings. In God's rules for living lies the key to His blessing upon our family, community and nation.
192 pages

## Father of Comfort

THE HIDDEN TREASURE
IN SUFFERING
Discovering blessings in the most unexpected situations. Shared from personal experience.
96 pages

FATHER OF COMFORT
Daily reflections on the God who cares.
160 pages

IN HIM WILL I TRUST
Gift book.
64 pages, 20 colour photos

## Father of Faithfulness

A FORETASTE OF HEAVEN
(American edition:
*I Found the Key to the Heart of God*)
Autobiography.
416 pages, 16 pages with photos

NATURE OUT OF CONTROL? —
WHEN GOD BREAKS HIS SILENCE
The assurance of God's unfailing love in an age of frequent natural disasters.
96 pages

MY FATHER, I TRUST YOU
*(quoted on p.137)*
Songs of trust and dedication.
64 pages